D0571752

ARMAGEDDON

Jimmy Swaggart

Jimmy Swaggart Ministries
P.O. Box 262550 • Baton Rouge, Louisiana 70826-2550
Website: www.jsm.org • Email: info@jsm.org
(225) 768-7000

ISBN 978-1-934655-71-9
09-116 • COPYRIGHT © 2011 World Evangelism Press®
12 13 14 15 16 17 18 19 20 21 22 23 / CW / 13 12 11 10 9 8 7 6 5 4 3 2 1

TABLE OF CONTENTS

INTRODUCTION

The word *"Armageddon"* is mentioned only one time in the Bible (Rev. 16:16). It is implied, however, any number of times.

There aren't many people in Christendom who aren't familiar with this word and what it implies. As well, it has come to be a synonym pertaining to catastrophe of unimagined proportion. In other words, there is nothing worse.

In addressing this subject, we do so with the realization that the actual event of Armageddon is nearer than ever. In other words, it is not just a throw-a-way word. It is an actual happening that's going to take place in the world in the near future, actually, in Israel proper. In fact, Israel is the flash point of the world at this time and has been for some years. However, the flash point, meaning that it could erupt into a conflagration, is more likely now than ever and, in fact, will conclude with *"Armageddon."* The Word of God alone gives us information as it regards this coming time. That coming time will present a battle that will be totally unlike anything that has ever happened on Planet Earth. It will be Satan's effort to completely annihilate the Jew, and in every capacity. It will be his effort to once and for all destroy every vestige of Jewish influence in the land that is now referred to as *"Israel."* He wants to erase that name from the face of the Earth. Armageddon will be his fell swoop.

THE BOOK OF REVELATION

While any number of Books in the Bible allude to this coming conflagration, it is the Book of Revelation that gives us by far the most information. In fact, Revelation tells us what the Great Tribulation will be and how it will conclude, which is the Battle of Armageddon.

Now, the Bible student must understand, Armageddon is not something that might happen or can be avoided if certain things are done, it is something that most definitely is going to take place. There is no doubt about that! At this stage, we do not know exactly when, but we know that it cannot be long in coming to pass.

The Book of Revelation in the Bible is little studied simply because most claim they cannot understand it. It is most difficult to understand! There is a reason for that.

The Book of Revelation, as it was given by the Holy Spirit to John the Beloved on the Isle of Patmos, where he was actually imprisoned, is given from the perspective of the spirit world. It, by and large, shows us what takes place in Glory before these happenings are brought to pass on Earth, whatever they might be. In other words, it shows us how that God orchestrates things on this Earth but without tampering with man's free moral agency. Due to the fact that the entirety of this Book is from the perspective of the spirit world is why it is so difficult to understand; however, admitting the difficulty, still, it can be understood. Considering how close we are to the fulfillment of these Bible Prophecies concerning the Endtime, Revelation should be on the must-study list. Unfortunately, not only does the world ignore it, even though it graphically spells out the near and the eternal future, sadder still, most of the church ignores it also.

ISRAEL

These ancient people called *"Jews,"* given their historical name of *"Israelites,"* or the modern name of *"Israelis,"* present a problem, which the world would much rather not address, but, in actuality, it has no choice.

Never before in history has a people been totally decimated and scattered all over the world, but yet, after nearly 2,000 years, has been brought together in a cohesive unit to form a Nation, and a powerful Nation at that. Such has never happened in history and could only happen now because the Lord is the One Who has done the doing. What He promised the Patriarchs, the Sages, and the Prophets of old, to be sure and certain, it will be carried out to the letter, and without fail.

As we go back in history, we find that Haman tried desperately to destroy these people. We find that Herod did the same thing, and we find that Hitler did all that he could to bring about the *"final solution,"* as he put it. Now, Israel faces her greatest test, actually, a catastrophe that will be even worse than the Holocaust. Jesus said so (Mat. 24:21). In other words, even though these ancient people are going to finally realize that which the Lord has proclaimed for them, which will take place in the coming Kingdom Age, the truth is, they are going to see some dark days before that time, as stated, the darkest they have ever known. The last great nemesis, the last great antagonist, will be the Antichrist, referred to as the *"Beast,"* or the *"man of sin."* This extremely charismatic individual, whom the Jews at first will think is their Messiah, will come closer than any of the antagonists of the past to destroying these ancient people. He will not succeed, but it will not be for a lack of trying. He will, he thinks, be the instigator of Armageddon. In his thinking, it will truly be the *"final solution."* But, in reality, it will be the Lord of Glory, the One Who is the Resurrection and the Life, the Son of the Living God, the Lord Jesus Christ Himself, Who will put the pieces together for that last great conflict, Armageddon. That's when the Antichrist will come to realize, but too late, that despite his power and despite the fact that Satan will have invested more in him than any other who has ever lived, in reality, he has only been a pawn in this great kaleidoscope of humanity.

ABRAHAM

The Jewish people had their beginning with Abraham. God called this man out of Ur of the Chaldees, which is modern day Iraq. It is amazing, as given to us in the Word of God, as to the number of Biblical things that have had, and do have, eternal consequences, which had their beginnings in Iraq. In the Bible, this area is referred to as Babylon, Babylonia, the Chaldees, Assyria, or Mesopotamia. Actually, the city of Babylon is mentioned more times in the Bible than any other city, with the exception of Jerusalem. The following might be of some interest:

- It is believed by some Bible scholars that the Garden of Eden was located where Babylon would later be built.
- Adam and Eve were created in Iraq.
- The first worship of the Lord took place in the Garden of Eden, which is in modern day Iraq.
- The first temptation occurred in Iraq.
- The terrible *"Fall"* occurred in Iraq.
- The Voice of the Lord was first heard in Iraq.
- The first sacrifices were offered in Iraq.
- The first recorded obedience of the Sacrificial Offerings, as it regarded Abel, took place in Iraq.
- The first refusal of God's Way, which was by virtue of the slain lamb, and carried out by Cain, took place in Iraq.
- The first murder took place in Iraq, with Cain killing his brother Abel.
- It is believed that Noah's Ark was built in Iraq.
- It was the Babylonian Empire, located in Iraq, which destroyed Judah and Jerusalem.
- The Book of Daniel in the Bible was written in Iraq.
- It is believed that the Antichrist will make his headquarters in Iraq.
- Incidentally, Iraq is the site of the first organized rebellion against God, as it regarded building the Tower of Babel.
- As well, the various languages of the world, instituted by the Lord, took place in Iraq.
- In one sense of the word, it all began in Iraq, and it all will end in Iraq.

THE PROMISE MADE TO ABRAHAM

As stated, the Jewish people began with Abraham, back to that Patriarch through Isaac. The Lord made promises to Abraham and, as well, to many of the Prophets. The following is taken directly from THE EXPOSITOR'S STUDY BIBLE, including the notes.

THE ABRAHAMIC COVENANT

"**Now the LORD had said unto Abram** *(referring to the Revelation, which had been given to the Patriarch a short time before; this Chapter is very important, for it records the first steps of this great Believer in the path of Faith)*, **Get you out of your country** *(separation)*, **and from your kindred** *(separation)*, **and from your father's house** *(separation)*, **unto a land that I will show you** *(refers to the fact that Abraham had no choice in the matter; he was to receive his orders from the Lord and go where those orders led him):*"

A GREAT NATION

"**And I will make of you a great Nation** *(the Nation which God made of Abraham has changed the world, and exists even unto this hour; in fact, this Nation, 'Israel,' still has a great part to play, which will take place in the coming Kingdom Age)*, **and I will bless you, and make your name great** *(according to Scripture, 'to bless' means 'to increase'; the builders of the Tower of Babel sought to 'make us a name,' whereas God took this man, who forsook all, and 'made his name great')*; **and you shall be a blessing:** *(Concerns itself with the greatest blessing of all. It is the glory of Abraham's Faith. God would give this man the meaning of Salvation, which is 'Justification by Faith,' which would come about through the Lord Jesus Christ, and what Christ would do on the Cross. Concerning this, Jesus said of Abraham, 'Your father Abraham rejoiced to see My Day: and he saw it, and was glad' [Jn. 8:56].)*"

THE BLESSING

"**And I will bless them who bless you** *(to bless Israel,* or any Believer, for that matter, guarantees the Blessings of God), **and curse him who curses you** (to curse Israel, or any Believer, guarantees that one will be cursed by God)**: and in you shall all families of the Earth be blessed.** (It speaks of Israel, which sprang from the loins of Abraham and the womb of Sarah, giving the world the Word of God and, more particularly, bringing the Messiah into the world. Through Christ, every family in the world who desires blessing from God can have that Blessing, i.e., 'Justification by Faith')**" (Gen. 12:1-3).**

THE BIRTH OF ISAAC

"And the LORD visited Sarah as He had said, and the LORD did unto Sarah as He had spoken (despite all of Satan's hindrances, Isaac, the progenitor and Type of the Messiah, is born)**.**

"For Sarah conceived, and bore Abraham a son in his old age, at the set time of which God had spoken to him. (Referring back to the past Chapter, if it be objected that this whole occurrence is incredible because no heathen prince would desire to marry a woman upwards of ninety years of age, or to conceive such a passion for her that to secure her he would murder her husband – the very fate which Abraham feared for himself – it may be replied that God must have miraculously renewed her youth, so that she became sufficiently youthful in appearance to suitably be desirable. Three times in these first two Verses, the clause points to the supernatural character of Isaac's birth.)**"**

ISAAC

"And Abraham called the name of his son that was born unto him, whom Sarah bore to him, Isaac. (The name means 'laughter.' It speaks of blessing, increase, healing, life, and well-being [Jn. 10:10]. As Isaac was a

*Type of Christ, it would not be wrong to say that one of the
names of Christ is 'laughter.')*

"**And Abraham circumcised his son Isaac being eight
days old, as God had commanded him** *(this was a sign of
the Covenant that God would ultimately send a Redeemer
into this world).*

"**And Abraham was an hundred years old, when
his son Isaac was born unto him** *(this Verse is placed in
the Text so that all may know that Isaac's birth was indeed
miraculous).*

"**And Sarah said, God has made me to laugh, so that
all who hear will laugh with me.** *(The mention of Sarah's
name some five times thus far in this Chapter is done for
purpose and reason; the Holy Spirit is impressing the fact
that Sarah was in truth the very mother of this miraculous
child. Sarah had once laughed in unbelief; she now laughs
in Faith, a laughter, incidentally, expressing joy, which will
never end. It all pointed to Christ. Because of Christ, untold
millions have laughed for joy.)*

"**And she said, Who would have said unto Abraham,
that Sarah should have given children suck? for I have
born him a son in his old age** *(this is a poem, and could
very well have been a song, and probably was).*

"**And the child grew, and was weaned** *(the custom
in those days was to nurse children for two or three years
before they were weaned; however, there is some indication
that Isaac was approximately five years old when he was
weaned)*: **and Abraham made a great feast the same day
that Isaac was weaned** *(at this time, the boy was turned
over to his father for training, at which time his education
began)*" **(Gen. 21:1-8).**

**We now come to the place of the rejection of Ishmael, who
was the son of the bondwoman, Hagar. This was the end result of
Abraham and Sarah resorting to the flesh, which brought forth
Ishmael, that which God would not recognize. As many know,**

the Arab world descended from Ishmael, i.e., the Muslims.

THE BONDWOMAN AND HER SON, ISHMAEL

"And Sarah saw the son of Hagar the Egyptian, which she had born unto Abraham, mocking. *(The effect of the birth of Isaac, a Work of the Holy Spirit, was to make manifest the character of Ishmael, a work of the flesh. The end result of the 'mocking' was that Ishmael actually desired to murder Isaac [Gal. 4:29]. Ishmael was probably eighteen to twenty years old at this time.)*

"Wherefore she said unto Abraham, Cast out this bondwoman and her son: *(Isaac and Ishmael symbolize the new and the old natures in the Believer. Hagar and Sarah typify the two Covenants of works and Grace, of bondage and liberty [Gal., Chpt. 4]. The birth of the new nature demands the expulsion of the old. It is impossible to improve the old nature. How foolish, therefore, appears the doctrine of moral evolution!)* for the son of this bond-woman shall not be heir with my son, even with Isaac. *(Allowed to remain, Ishmael would murder Isaac; allowed to remain, the flesh will murder the Spirit. The Divine way of holiness is to 'put off the old man,' just as Abraham 'put off Ishmael.'*

"*Man's way of holiness is to improve the 'old man,' that is, to improve Ishmael. The effort is foolish and hopeless.)*"

THE STRUGGLE OF ABRAHAM

"And the thing was very grievous in Abraham's sight because of his son. *(It is always a struggle to cast out this element of bondage, that is, salvation by works, of which this is a type. For legalism is dear to the heart. Ishmael was the fruit, and, to Abraham, the fair fruit of his own energy and planning, which God can never accept.)*

"And God said unto Abraham, Let it not be grievous

in your sight because of the lad, and because of your bondwoman; in all that Sarah has said unto you, hearken unto her voice; for in Isaac shall your seed be called. *(It is labor lost to seek to make a crooked thing straight. Hence, all efforts after the improvement of nature are utterly futile, so far as God is concerned. The 'flesh' must go, which typifies the personal ability, strength, and efforts of the Believer. The Faith of the Believer must be entirely in Christ and what Christ has done at the Cross. Then, and then alone, can the Holy Spirit have latitude to work in our lives, bringing forth perpetual victory [Rom. 6:14]. It must ever be understood, 'in Isaac [in Christ] shall your seed be called')"* **(Gen. 21:9-12).**

BECAUSE OF ABRAHAM, ISHMAEL WAS ALSO TO BE BLESSED

"And also of the son of the bondwoman *(Ishmael)* **will I make a nation, because he is your seed** *(out of this 'work of the flesh' ultimately came the religion of Islam, which claims that Ishmael is the promised seed, and not Isaac)"* **(Gen. 21:13).**

So, the Scripture and notes we have just given proclaim the beginning of that which is the bone of contention throughout the entirety of the world at this present time. It is fastly coming to a head and, in fact, will have its conclusion in the coming Great Tribulation. In essence, and in a sense, it will conclude with *"Armageddon."*

Israel presently sits in a sea of Muslims. This little country is only about the size of the State of New Jersey. There are about six million Jews in the State of Israel, surrounded by over one hundred million Muslims, regarding the Middle East, with over a billion Muslims worldwide.

So, Israel faces the threats of Ahmadinejad of Iran and, as well, the animosity of the United Nations. And then, beyond all of that, and far more important, the Obama Administration seems to be not at all in sympathy with Israel in any capacity. In fact, her problems will only increase until the Antichrist comes on the scene, who Israel, in her deception, will accept as her Messiah. Other than crucifying Christ, this will be the biggest mistake that she will have ever made.

What the world is dealing with here is the oldest contention on the face of the Earth, as we've stated, having begun with Abraham. That was some 4,000 years ago. It is now coming to a head. In fact, one might say, and not be too far off base, that this question, this contention, just might be the most important situation on the face of the Earth at this present time.

GOD'S PROPHETIC TIME CLOCK

If one wants to know how late it is, prophetically speaking, one only has to look at Israel. They are God's Prophetic Time Clock. It is obvious that this time is about up.

Some have claimed that the Lord has another method of Salvation for the Jews than He does the balance of the world. That is gross error! Jesus said, which leaves no room for argument:

"**I am the Way, the Truth, and the Life** *(proclaims in no uncertain terms exactly Who and What Jesus is)*: **no man comes unto the Father, but by Me** *(He declares positively that this idea of God as Father, this approach to God for every man is through Him – through what He is and what He has done, which speaks of Calvary)*" **(Jn. 14:6).**

Armageddon constitutes the head. In other words, everything will come to a head in the battle referred to as Armageddon. This will solve the Jewish question, the question regarding the Antichrist, and, in fact, the entirety of the world. The reason is simple. The Second Coming, which will be the most cataclysmic event the world has ever known, will take place during the Battle of Armageddon. Then the man of sin will see just

Who the Lord Jesus Christ actually is, and What He can do. In fact, at that time, the entirety of the world will see by television exactly what is to take place. There will be no doubt about it. The eyes of most of the world will be fixed upon this spot in tiny Israel, and then every question will be answered.

CHAPTER ONE

THE FUTURE OF PLANET EARTH

Some of the prognosticators do not speak very positively at all concerning the future of this Planet. Some claim that global warming is going to take a deadly toll. Others say that the opposite will happen, and I refer to another so-called Ice Age.

And then, we have the climate conditions, which, in the recent past, have been worse than have ever been recorded. While there have always been storms, tornadoes, earthquakes, etc., the frequency and ferocity of that, which is presently happening, has taken it to a new level.

What is happening?

The Apostle Paul, after a fashion, addressed this situation. He said:

THE EARNEST EXPECTATION OF THE CREATION

"For the earnest expectation of the creature *(should have been translated, 'for the earnest expectation of the Creation')* waits for the manifestation of the sons of God *(pertains to the coming Resurrection of Life)*.

"For the creature *(Creation)* was made subject to

vanity *(Adam's Fall signaled the fall of Creation)*, **not willingly** *(the Creation did not sin, even as such cannot sin, but became subject to the result of sin, which is death)*, **but by reason of Him Who has subjected** *the same* **in** Hope *(speaks of God as the One Who passed sentence because of Adam's Fall but, at the same time, gave us a 'Hope'; that 'Hope' is Christ, Who will rectify all things)*,

"**Because the creature** *(Creation)* **itself also shall be delivered** *(presents this 'Hope' as effecting that Deliverance, which He did by the Cross)* **from the bondage of corruption** *(speaks of mortality, i.e., 'death')* **into the glorious liberty of the Children of God** *(when man fell, Creation fell! when man shall be delivered, Creation will be delivered, as well, and is expressed in the word 'also')*."

THE GROANING OF CREATION

"**For we know that the whole Creation** *(everything has been affected by Satan's rebellion and Adam's Fall)* **groans and travails in pain together until now** *(refers to the common longing of the elements of the Creation to be brought back to their original perfection)*."

WAITING FOR THE ADOPTION

"**And not only** *they* *(the Creation and all it entails)*, **but ourselves also** *(refers to Believers)*, **who have the Firstfruits of the Spirit** *(even though Jesus addressed every single thing lost in the Fall at the Cross, we only have a part of that possession now, with the balance coming at the Resurrection)*, **even we ourselves groan within ourselves** *(proclaims the obvious fact that all Jesus paid for in the Atonement has not yet been fully realized)*, **waiting for the Adoption** *(should be translated, 'waiting for the fulfillment of the process, which Adoption into the Family of God guarantees')*, *to wit,* **the Redemption of our body** *(the* *glorifying of our physical body that will take place at the Resurrection)*" **(Rom. 8:19-23).**

TWO REASONS FOR THE CLIMATE DISTURBANCES

There are two major reasons, I believe, for the increase in climate disturbances, which have wreaked havoc over great parts of the Planet. It has nothing to do with El Nino or other similarities. The two reasons are *"failure to preach the Cross"* and *"the last of the last days"*:

FAILURE TO PREACH THE CROSS

The Cross of Christ is God's Answer to the sin question, and God's only Answer to the sin question. Paul wrote:

> **"But this Man** *(this Priest, Christ Jesus)***, after He had offered One Sacrifice for sins forever** *(speaks of the Cross)***, sat down on the Right Hand of God** *(refers to the great contrast with the Priests under the Levitical system, who never sat down because their work was never completed; the Work of Christ was a 'Finished Work,' and needed no repetition)*;
> **"From henceforth expecting till His enemies be made His Footstool.** *(These enemies are Satan and all fallen Angels and demon spirits, plus all who follow Satan)*" **(Heb. 10:12-13).**

The major message preached by the Apostle Paul was the Cross (I Cor. 1:23). He was given the meaning of the New Covenant, which is the Cross of Christ, and was made the masterbuilder of the Church by the Holy Spirit. In other words, the Cross of Christ was the Foundation of all that he preached. If it's not the foundation of all that we preach presently, then whatever it is we are preaching may be about the Gospel, but it's really not the Gospel. Paul told us what the Gospel actually is by saying:

"Christ sent me not to baptize, but to preach the Gospel: not with wisdom of words, lest the Cross of Christ should be made of none effect" (I Cor. 1:17).

My contention is, if preachers would once again begin to preach the Cross, which is the only thing that holds back the Judgment of God, this, I believe, would greatly lessen the climate disturbances. While it certainly would not end them altogether, I do believe it would have a very positive effect in the frequency and the ferocity. But yet, I do not labor under any illusion that this is going to be done. Hopeful, yes! But that's about as far as I can go. Please note the following:

• The Cross of Christ is the only thing standing between mankind and eternal Hell.

• The Cross of Christ is the only thing standing between the Church and apostasy.

• The Cross of Christ is the only thing that holds back the Judgment of God.

Were it not for the Cross, God could not even look at us, much less, have communion with us. It is the Cross which opened up the way to the very Throne of God. Please note the following very carefully:

II Samuel, Chapter 24, records David's sin in taking a national census in an unscriptural way.

Without going into detail, the Scripture says:

"So the LORD sent a pestilence upon Israel from the morning even until the time appointed: and there died of the people from Dan even to Beer-sheba seventy thousand men" (II Sam. 24:15). As would be obvious, this was a staggering number of men who died instantly, especially considering how small that Israel actually was.

Then the Scripture says, *"And when the Angel stretched out his hand upon Jerusalem to destroy it, the LORD repented Him of the evil, and said to the Angel that destroyed the people, It is enough: stay now your hand. And the Angel of the LORD was by the threshingplace of Araunah the Jebusite"* (II Sam. 24:16).

But then, the Lord sent Gad the Prophet to David:

"**. . . and said unto him, Go up, rear an Altar unto the LORD in the threshingfloor of Araunah the Jebusite** *(the only answer for sin, and I mean the only answer, is the 'Altar,' i.e., 'the Cross,' of which the Altar was a Type)*" **(II Sam. 24:18).**

And then the Scripture said:

"**And David built there an Altar unto the LORD, and offered Burnt Offerings and Peace Offerings. So the LORD was intreated for the land, and the plague was stayed from Israel.** *(There is a 'plague' called 'sin' that is destroying this world and causing multiple hundreds of millions to be eternally lost. There's only one cure for that plague, and that is the precious, atoning, Vicarious Offering of the Blood of the Lord Jesus Christ, which was done at the Cross, and our acceptance of Him. All the churches in the world will never stay the 'plague.' All the good works, good intentions, money, religion, prestige, or education will not stop this plague of sin. Only the precious Blood of Jesus Christ can, here symbolized by the 'Altar' – 'and the plague was stayed')*" **(II Sam. 24:25).**

Let me say it again! If preachers would begin to preach the Cross, this *"plague,"* if not stopped altogether, would be seriously slowed in this nation, and even the entirety of the world. Preach the Cross!

THE LAST OF THE LAST DAYS

We have already alluded to the following but please allow me to explain it further. When Adam fell in the Garden of Eden, the Creation, in some way, fell also. Of course, such is inanimate, but, still, it means that the Creation doesn't function as God originally intended for it to function. That's the reason for all the tornadoes, earthquakes, famines, droughts, hurricanes, etc. In a sense, all of this means that *". . . the whole Creation groans and travails in pain together until now"* (Rom. 8:22). In the coming Kingdom Age when things will have been set right, there will be no more storms, earthquakes, hurricanes, etc.

The inclement weather patterns that the world is now experiencing, which means an increase, as previously stated, in frequency and intensity, is a sign that we are nearing the end.

This doesn't mean the end of the world because the world will never end, but it does mean the end of the Church Age, which will usher in the coming Kingdom Age when Christ will rule Personally from Jerusalem. However, there is a transition between the Church Age and the coming Kingdom Age called the *"Great Tribulation."* This period of time, which will run seven or more years, will experience a convulsion such as it has never known before in all of its history. As it regards this particular period of time, Jesus said:

> "For then shall be great tribulation *(the last three and one half years of the seven-year period)*, such as was not since the beginning of the world to this time, no, nor ever shall be *(the worst the world has ever known, and will be so bad that it will never be repeated)*.
>
> "And except those days should be shortened, there should no flesh be saved *(refers to Israel coming close to extinction)*: but for the elect's *(Israel's)* sake those days shall be shortened *(by the Second Coming)*" (Mat. 24:21-22).

In fact, during the seven-year Great Tribulation, climate conditions are going to be worse than ever. There will be earthquakes that will be greater and more destructive than the world has ever previously known. Concerning this, the Scripture says:

> "And I beheld when He *(Christ)* had opened the sixth Seal, and, lo, there was a great earthquake *(the*

first of several); **and the sun became black as sackcloth of hair** *(probably caused by dust filling the air due to the earthquake)*, **and the moon became as blood** *(doesn't mean the moon was actually turned to blood, but that it 'became as blood,' again, probably referring to the dust particles filling the air)*;

"**And the stars of Heaven fell unto the earth** *(refers to meteorites or shooting stars)*, **even as a fig tree casts her untimely figs, when she is shaken of a mighty wind.** *(There will be a bombardment on the earth of these meteorites, which will cause untold damage.)*

"**And the Heaven departed as a scroll when it is rolled together** *(pertains to the shaking of the heavens, which insti-gates the meteorites)*; **and every mountain and island were moved out of their places.** *(This proclaims power of unimagined proportions. The greater thrust will more than likely be in the Middle East)*" **(Rev. 6:12-14).**

The Scripture then says:

"**And the Angel took the Censer, and filled it with fire of the Altar** *(this is the Brazen Altar in Heaven that typi-fied the Death of our Lord, which was necessary in order that man might be redeemed; as is obvious here, Heaven is filled with the portrayal of that Sacrificial, Atoning Death)*, **and cast *it* into the earth** *(with the Salvation of the Cross being rejected by the Earth, the Judgment of the Cross will now commence)*: **and there were voices, and thunderings, and lightnings, and an earthquake.** *(All of this speaks of the fact that it is Judgment coming, and Judgment such as the world has never seen before)*" **(Rev. 8:5).**

"**And the same hour was there a great earthquake** *(this is one of five times that earthquakes are mentioned; it is the last one that will take place and happens under the seventh Vial, which is at the very conclusion of the Great Tribulation)*, **and the tenth part of the city fell** *(refers to*

Jerusalem), **and in the earthquake were slain of men seven thousand: and the remnant were affrighted, and gave Glory to the God of Heaven.** *(There is some indication in the Greek Text that some of these people gave their hearts to Christ)"* **(Rev. 11:13).**

THE LORD JESUS CHRIST

If it is to be remembered, our Lord predicted that earthquakes and other similar things would happen to a greater degree as the end approaches, and more particularly, in the coming Great Tribulation, as we've already noted (Lk. 21:11).

DANIEL

Daniel, the Prophet/Statesman, some 500 years before Christ, predicted that the Great Tribulation would last for seven years, with the last three and a half years being the worst. He said:

"And he shall confirm the covenant with many for one week: and in the midst of the week he shall cause the sacrifice and the oblation to cease, and for the overspreading of abominations he shall make it desolate, even until the consummation, and that determined shall be poured upon the desolate. *('And he shall confirm,' refers to the Antichrist. The phrase, 'And in the midst of the week,' refers to three and a half years, at which time the Antichrist will show his true colors and stop the sacrifices in the newly-built Temple. At that time, he will actually invade Israel, with her suffering her first military defeat since her formation as a Nation in 1948.*

"'Even until the consummation,' means until the end of the seven-year Great Tribulation period. The phrase, 'And that determined shall be poured upon the desolate,' refers to all the Prophecies being fulfilled regarding the great suffering that Israel will go through the last three

and a half years of the Great Tribulation [Mat. 24:21-22])" **(Dan. 9:27).**

ISRAEL'S REJECTION OF CHRIST

When Israel rejected Christ at His First Advent, this consigned the entirety of this Planet to now some 2,000 years of continued wars, troubles, and disturbances.

John the Baptist, who was the forerunner of Christ, actually, the one chosen to introduce Christ, and who was the first Prophet in Israel in some 400 years, began his ministry

". . . preaching in the wilderness of Judaea;

"And saying, Repent you: for the Kingdom of Heaven *(Kingdom from the Heavens, headed up by Jesus Christ)* is at hand *(was being offered to Israel).*

"For this is he *(John the Baptist)* who was spoken of by the Prophet Isaiah, saying, The voice of one crying in the wilderness, Prepare you the Way of the LORD, make His Paths straight *(Isa. 40:3)*" (Mat. 3:1-3).

As stated, John preceded Christ by a few months.
When Jesus came, His Message was basically the same:

". . . Repent: for the Kingdom of Heaven is at hand *(the Kingdom from Heaven, headed up by Christ, for the purpose of reestablishing the Kingdom of God over the Earth; the Kingdom was rejected by Israel)*" **(Mat. 4:17).**

In other words, the Kingdom was offered to Israel at that time, but Israel refused it. One must understand, to refuse the King, Who is the Lord Jesus Christ, is, at the same time, to refuse the Kingdom.

THE KINGDOM

Of course, it is a moot point; however, if Israel had accepted

Him as their King, Messiah and Saviour, how would the Plan of Redemption have been carried out?

One must understand, if it was not possible to accept the Kingdom at that time, it would not have been offered to them by John the Baptist and, especially, by our Lord. Of course, the Lord knew through foreknowledge that Israel would reject Him and, thereby, reject the Kingdom.

To answer the question as it regards Redemption, which required the Cross, if Israel had accepted Him, to be sure, Rome was waiting in the wings, and in no way would they have tolerated another King. They would have crucified Him.

The point I wish to make is, when the Kingdom was offered to Israel, as it had to be because they were God's Chosen People, their rejecting it plunged this Planet into a continuing time frame of trouble, war, and heartache that has now lasted for some 2,000 years. Jesus addressed this in His last Sermon, which was on the Mount of Olives that took place hours before His Crucifixion. Ironically enough, the Lord began His Ministry with a *"Sermon on the Mount"* (Mat., Chpt. 5), and closed it with a *"Sermon on the Mount"* (Mat., Chpt. 24). The first mountain was in Galilee, the second mountain, which was the Mount of Olives, was in Jerusalem.

Knowing that Israel had rejected Him, which means that they were, by and large, consigning themselves to destruction, He gave a kaleidoscopic account of what this rejection would mean as far as Israel was concerned, the Work of God was concerned, and this Planet was concerned. The Scripture says:

SIGNS OF THE ENDTIME

"And as He sat upon the Mount of Olives *(the coming siege of Jerusalem by the Romans some thirty-seven years later, began at this exact spot where Christ was sitting)*, the Disciples came unto Him privately *(out of earshot of the many Pilgrims in the city for the Passover)*, saying, Tell us, when shall these things be? *(Has to do here with*

*the utterance He had just given concerning the destruc-
tion of the Temple.)* **and what** *shall be* **the sign of Your
Coming** *(refers to the Second Coming, which has not yet
taken place)*, **and of the end of the world?** *(Should have
been translated 'age,' because the world will never end.)*"

DECEPTION

"**And Jesus answered and said unto them** *(will now
give the future of Israel and how it will effect the entirety
of the world)*, **Take heed that no man deceive you** *(places
deception as Satan's greatest weapon)*.

"**For many shall come in My Name** *(concerns itself
primarily with the time immediately before the coming
Great Tribulation, and especially its first half)*, **saying, I
am Christ; and shall deceive many** *(the greatest of these
will be the Antichrist, who will claim to be the Messiah)*.

"**And you shall hear of wars and rumours of wars**
*(has abounded from the beginning but will accelerate dur-
ing the first half of the Great Tribulation)*: **see that you
be not troubled** *(concerns true Believers)*: **for all** *these
things* **must come to pass** *(we are very near presently to
the beginning of fulfillment of what Jesus said)*, **but the
end is not yet** *(the end will be at the Second Coming)*."

WARS AND GREAT TROUBLES

"**For nation shall rise against nation, and kingdom
against kingdom: and there shall be famines, and pes-
tilences, and earthquakes, in divers places** *(few places in
the world, if any, will be exempt from these Judgments)*.

"**All these** *are* **the beginning of sorrows** *(first half of the
Great Tribulation)*.

"**Then shall they deliver you up to be afflicted, and shall
kill you** *(pertains to the mid-point of the Great Tribulation
when the Antichrist, whom Israel thought was the Messiah,*

will show his true colors): **and you shall be hated of all nations for My Name's sake** *(no nation will come to her rescue; Israel hates Christ, but Christ is the reason that the world hates Israel).*

"And then shall be many be offended *(some Jews will accept Christ, which will be an offense to others)*, **and shall betray one another, and shall hate one another** *(the Jews who accept Christ will be the brunt of this animosity)."*

FALSE PROPHETS

"And many false prophets shall rise, and shall deceive many *(they will help the Antichrist).*

"And because iniquity shall abound *(the Antichrist called 'the man of sin' [II Thess. 2:3])*, **the love of many shall wax cold** *(some who accept Christ will turn their backs on Him).*

"But he who shall endure unto the end *(refers to the end of the Great Tribulation)*, **the same shall be saved** *(speaks of survival and not the Salvation of the soul).*

"And this Gospel of the Kingdom *(refers to the same type of Gospel preached by Christ and Paul)* **shall be preached in all the world for a witness unto all nations** *(not every person, but to all nations; this is close presently to being fulfilled)*; **and then shall the end come** *(the Second Coming)"* **(Mat. 24:3-14).**

THE ABOMINATION OF DESOLATION

If it is to be noticed, this Olivet discourse has to do with Israel. So, in a sense, the Church is, by and large, omitted, with only the reference of the Gospel of the Kingdom being preached in all the world, etc. If it is to be remembered, the Disciples asked Him a question concerning the Endtime respecting Israel. At that time, they really had no knowledge of the Church. So, Jesus answered them according to what they had asked.

While He alluded to this now some 2,000-year span, it was only to mention the fact that wars would continue and great troubles and difficulties, etc. But most of His Statements concerned the coming Great Tribulation. In fact, He now goes to the mid-point of that coming terrible time and says:

"When you therefore shall see the abomination of desolation, spoken of by Daniel the Prophet, stand in the Holy Place *(speaks of the Antichrist invading Israel and taking over the Temple)*, (whoso reads, let him understand:) *(Reads it in the Word of God [Dan. 8:9-14; 9:27; 11:45; 12:1, 7, 11].)*

"Then let them who be in Judaea flee into the mountains *(when the Antichrist invades Israel at the mid-point of the Great Tribulation)*:

"Let him who is on the housetop not come down to take any thing out of his house *(houses are flat on top in that part of the world; during the summer, people often sleep on top of the house; speaks of the necessity of haste)*:

"Neither let him who is in the field return back to take his clothes.

"And woe unto them who are with child, and to them who give suck in those days! *(The necessity of fleeing will be so urgent that it will be difficult for pregnant women and mothers with little babies.)*

"But pray you that your flight be not in winter *(bad weather)*, neither on the Sabbath Day *(concerns the strict religious observance of the Sabbath, doesn't permit travel)*:"

THE GREAT TRIBULATION

"For then shall be great tribulation *(the last three and one half years)*, such as was not since the beginning of the world to this time, no, nor ever shall be *(the worst the world has ever known and will be so bad that it will never be repeated)*.

"And except those days should be shortened, there should no flesh be saved *(refers to Israel coming close to extinction)*: but for the elect's *(Israel's)* sake those days shall be shortened *(by the Second Coming)*.

"Then if any man shall say unto you, Lo, here *is* Christ, or there; believe *it* not *(don't be deceived)*.

"For there shall arise false Christs, and false prophets *(the Antichrist and the false prophet [Rev., Chpt. 13])*, and shall show great signs and wonders *(which will be offered as proof)*; insomuch that, if *it were* possible, they shall deceive the very elect *(will attempt to deceive Israel)*.

"Behold, I have told you before *(is meant to emphasize the seriousness of the matter)*.

"Wherefore if they shall say unto you, Behold, he is in the desert; go not forth; behold, *he is* in the secret chambers; believe *it* not *(the next Verse will tell the manner of His Coming, which will eclipse all pretenders)*.

THE COMING OF THE SON OF MAN

"For as the lightning comes out of the east, and shines even unto the west *(is meant to proclaim the most cataclysmic event the world has ever known)*; so shall also the coming of the Son of Man be *(no one will have to ask, is this really Christ; it will be overly obvious)*.

"For wheresoever the carcase is *(speaks of the Battle of Armageddon)*, there will the eagles be gathered together *(should have been translated, 'there will the vultures be gathered together' [refers to Ezek. 39:17])*.

"Immediately after the tribulation of those days *(speaks of the time immediately preceding the Second Coming)* shall the sun be darkened, and the moon shall not give her light *(the light of these orbs will be dim by comparison to the light of the Son of God)*, and the stars shall fall from Heaven *(a display of heavenly fireworks at the Second Coming)*, and the powers of the Heavens shall be shaken *(will work with the Son of God against the Antichrist at the Second Coming):*

"And then shall appear the sign of the Son of Man in Heaven *(pertains to the Second Coming, which will take place in the midst of these Earth and Heaven shaking events):* **and then shall all the tribes of the Earth mourn** *(concerns all the nations of the world, which possibly will see this phenomenon by television)*, **and they shall see the Son of Man** *(denotes Christ and His Human, Glorified Body)* **coming in the clouds of Heaven with Power and great Glory** *(lends credence to the thought that much of the world will see Him by television as He makes His Descent).*

"And He shall send His Angels *(they will be visible)* **with a great sound of a trumpet** *(announcing the gathering of Israel)*, **and they shall gather together His Elect** *(Israel)* **from the four winds, from one end of Heaven to the other** *(Jews will be gathered from all over the world and brought to Israel)"* **(Mat. 24:15-31).**

Now the Lord gives us a clue as to when all of this is going to take place. He said:

THE PARABLE OF THE FIG TREE

"Now learn a Parable of the fig tree *(the Bible presents three trees, the fig, the olive, and the vine, as representing the Nation of Israel, nationally, spiritually, and dispensationally)*; **When his branch is yet tender, and puts forth leaves** *(is meant to serve as the illustration of Israel nationally)*, **you know that summer *is* near** *(refers to Israel as the greatest Prophetic Sign of all, telling us that we are now living in the last of the Last Days)*;

"So likewise you *(points to the modern church)*, **when you shall see all these things** *(which we are now seeing as it regards Israel)*, **know that it is near, *even* at the doors** *(the fulfillment of Endtime Prophecies).*

"Verily I say unto you, This generation shall not pass *(the generation of Jews which will be alive at the beginning of the Great Tribulation; as well, it was a prediction by Christ that irrespective of the problems that Israel would face, even from His Day, they would survive)*, **till all these things be fulfilled** *(there is no doubt, they will be fulfilled)*.

"Heaven and Earth shall pass away *(doesn't refer to annihilation, but rather a change from one condition or state to another)*, but My Words shall not pass away *(what the Word of God says, will be!)*.

"But of that day and hour knows no *man*, no, not the Angels of Heaven, but My Father only" (Mat. 24:32-36).

Verse 36 plainly tells us that no man should try to put a date on the Rapture of the Church or even the events here as it regards the Second Coming.

When the Great Tribulation begins, which will commence when the Antichrist signs the seven-year agreement with Israel and the Muslim world, then it will be possible to tell what is going to happen simply because it is amply illustrated in the Book of Revelation. In other words, we know that the Battle of Armageddon will take place at the end of the Great Tribulation and that Jesus Christ will come back during that Battle. But as to exactly when all of this takes place, we do not now know; however, we do have a clue.

As we have said in the above notes, Israel is likened by Christ to the *"fig tree."* He then said, *"When his branch is yet tender, and puts forth leaves . . ."* (Mat. 24:32). All of this pertains to Israel once again becoming a Nation in 1948 and of her troubles and difficulties, which have followed that time, even unto the present. As previously stated, Israel is God's Prophetic Time Clock. In other words, if we want to know how late it is, we need only look at Israel. This tells us that it is very late. The Dispensation of the Church is about at an end. This will be followed by the Great Tribulation, which Tribulation will pertain to the whole world, but, more than all, to Israel.

NATIONS OF THE WORLD AND
THE POWERS OF DARKNESS

Daniel, the great Prophet/Statesman, gave us insight into the spirit world, as it regards nations and empires, as no other. Paul mentioned it but didn't go into any detail at all. To set the stage, we'll address Paul first.

PAUL THE APOSTLE

He said, *"For we wrestle not against flesh and blood, but against principalities, against powers, against the rulers of the darkness of this world, against spiritual wickedness in high places"* (Eph. 6:12).

There are four designations listed in this Scripture. They are:

1. *"Principalities:"* the Greek word for *"principalities"* is *"Archas,"* and means, *"powerful fallen angels who threw in their lot with Lucifer at the revolution ages past."*

2. *"Powers:"* the Greek word for *"powers"* is *"exousias,"* which means *"authorities, those who derive their power from and execute the will of the chief rulers."* In other words, they answer to the *"Principalities,"* who answer to Satan.

These *"Principalities"* concern themselves with particular areas of the Earth, over which they have control. The *"Powers"* are the fallen Angels who carry out that control. In other words, they are the *"authorities in the spirit realm,"* who bring about the desired results of Satan, with the responsibility entrusted to the *"Principalities."*

3. *"Rulers of the darkness of this world:"* these are those who carry out the instructions of the *"Powers."* The Greek word for *"rulers"* is *"kosmokrapopas,"* which speaks of *"spirit world-rulers"* (Dan. 10:13-21; Eph. 1:21; 6:12; Col. 1:16-18). These are *"Rulers"* under the *"Powers,"* who, as stated, are under the *"Principalities,"* who are under *"Satan."*

4. *"Spiritual wickedness in high places:"* this refers to demon spirits. The Greek words are, *"pneumatika ponerias,"* which

means, *"that of the wicked spirits of Satan,"* i.e., *"demon spirits."*

The words *"high places"* do not refer to Heaven or heavenly places, but rather the lower heavens, the lower atmosphere surrounding this Earth. That's what the Holy Spirit through Paul is speaking about when he referred to Satan as *". . . the prince of the power of the air . . ."* (Eph. 2:2).

As we have stated, the other three designations are fallen Angels, while the last designation refers exclusively to demon spirits. We know that the fallen Angels were originally holy and righteous before God and remained that way until their fall. However, we have no clue in the Word of God, at least of substantial note, which tells us of the origin of demons. This we do know, God did not originally create them in this fashion.

PREADAMITE CREATION

Some scholars believe they were inhabitants of this Earth before the fall of Lucifer (not the Fall of Adam and Eve), and that they threw in their lot with Lucifer at the time of his rebellion against God. While I make no claims at being a Bible scholar, I, as well, do subscribe to this interpretation. As a result, this creation, whatever it was, became disembodied, thereby, seeking a body to inhabit, before they will be eternally consigned to the Lake of Fire.

Satan rules his kingdom of darkness on this Earth (and it is confined to this Earth), through these four designations. Human beings have no contact with fallen Angels, except possibly with Satan himself; however, the entirety of the human race has contact with demon spirits constantly. In fact, all unbelievers are controlled more or less by demon spirits, with some actually being possessed.

FALLEN ANGELS AND DEMON SPIRITS

All Christians face these spirits of darkness (demons) constantly, even as Paul is explaining here. While he mentions all four designations, the first three (fallen Angels) are involved in the carrying out of the plans of Satan, with, it seems, demon spirits alone making direct contact with human beings.

In fact, there is no mention of fallen Angels, except Satan, in the Ministry of Christ or in the Acts of the Apostles respecting the Early Church. It was all with demon spirits, even as it is presently.

It seems that the fallen Angels under Satan formulate the stratagems and plans respecting the kingdom of darkness in its opposition against Believers. However, it seems that they do not involve themselves directly with humans, that being the task of demon spirits (Dan. 10:13, 20).

DANIEL'S VISION

Insight into the spirit world, which Daniel here portrays to us, is amazing indeed! In a sense, this is what the Apostle Paul was speaking of, although he did not go into any detail. Paul's Ministry was not so much Prophecy as it was the meaning of the New Covenant, which is the meaning of the Cross. As it regards Daniel, he was given a greater insight into Endtime events, which will affect the entirety of the world, but more so Israel, than any other Prophet.

The narrative that I will give is taken directly from THE EXPOSITOR'S STUDY BIBLE. We will pick it up in the middle of a Vision given to Daniel by the Lord. Even though the Scripture at this point does not particularly state such, it is almost certain that this was the Angel Gabriel speaking to Daniel. The Scripture says:

> "Then said he unto me, Fear not, Daniel: for from the first day that you did set your heart to understand, and to chasten yourself before your God, your words were heard, and I am come for your words. (*'For from the first day,' speaks of his petition to God and his effort to understand God's Purpose concerning His People. Then*

God commissioned Gabriel to come to him.)

"But the prince of the kingdom of Persia withstood me one and twenty days: but, lo, Michael, one of the Chief Princes, came to help me; and I remained there with the kings of Persia. *('The prince of the kingdom of Persia,' refers to an evil Angel appointed by Satan to control the Persian government, which, of course, was done without the knowledge of its earthly king. This Passage appears to reveal that Satan places an agent in charge of every nation [fallen Angel]; and, if so, this may explain national hatreds and national movements.*

'Similarly, God has His Angelic Agents operating in opposition to Satan's. The conflict of Eph., Chpt. 6, to which we have briefly alluded, and the Battle of Rev., Chpt. 12, harmonize with this supposition.)"

SUBJECT OF THE VISION

"Now I am come to make you understand what shall befall your people in the latter days: for yet the Vision is for many days. *('What shall befall your people,' refers solely to the Jews [9:24; 12:1]. Therefore, the Gentile nations are included, but only as they affect Israel, and only as Israel is ensconced in her land and offering sacrifices in the Temple; in fact, this Temple will soon be built.)*

"And when he had spoken such words unto me, I set my face toward the ground, and I became dumb. *(Quite possibly, the many times mentioned concerning the Vision being fulfilled in the 'latter days' is because Daniel may have thought that these things would happen shortly, with Israel ultimately being restored to her place and position of power and supremacy; however, that was not the case.)*

"And, behold, one like the similitude of the sons of men touched my lips: then I opened my mouth, and spoke, and said unto Him Who stood before me, O my Lord, by the Vision my sorrows are turned upon me, and I have

retained no strength. *(Quite possibly, this was Christ, because Daniel addressed Him as 'O my Lord!')*

"For how can the servant of this my Lord talk with this my Lord? for as for me, straightway there remained no strength in me, neither is there breath left in me. *(The implication is that it is not the Vision alone causing the physical weakness, but rather the very Presence of Christ.)*

"Then there came again and touched me one like the appearance of a man, and he strengthened me,

"And said, O man greatly beloved, fear not: peace be unto you, be strong, yes, be strong. And when He had spoken unto me, I was strengthened, and said, Let my Lord speak; for You have strengthened me. *(It seems that this is the Lord in a pre-incarnate appearance, actually speaking to Daniel.)*

THE PRINCE OF GRECIA

"Then said He, Know you wherefore I come unto you? and now will I return to fight with the prince of Persia: and when I am gone forth, lo, the prince of Grecia shall come. *(It seems that now Gabriel once again picks up the conversation. 'And now will I return to fight with the prince of Persia,' did not mean that he would leave immediately, but, when the Vision was completed, he would resume the conflict with this satanic prince.*

"'And when I am gone forth, lo, the prince of Grecia shall come,' refers to Gabriel ultimately being successful in this conflict, allowing the satanic prince to bring in the Grecian Empire. This would take place less than 200 years in the future.

"The 'prince of Grecia' is not an earthly prince, but, instead, a fallen Angel working under the direct instructions of Satan, who would control the Grecian Empire when it did come into being. It was this evil prince which helped Alexander the Great conquer the known world of

that day, although without his knowledge. This 'prince' is now confined to the underworld, but will be released in the last days in order to help the Antichrist [Rev. 7:8-14].

"It is the same presently, with fallen Angels controlling entire nations [Eph. 6:12].)

MICHAEL AND GABRIEL

"But I will show you that which is noted in the Scripture of Truth: and there is none who holds with me in these things, but Michael your prince. *('The Scripture of Truth' refers to the dream originally given to Nebuchadnezzar [Dan. 2:39], which showed these empires, as well as the two Visions already given to Daniel, as noted in Dan. 7:5-6 and Dan. 8:3-8. 'And there is none who holds with me in these things, but Michael your prince,' denotes the truth that as these fallen Angels reigned supreme over certain empires, Michael served in the same position over Israel and, in fact, still does!)*" **(Dan. 10:12-21).**

The following is extremely important simply because it deals with the fallen Angel who helped Alexander the Great, and who will help the Antichrist when he takes power, which will be in the near future.

FROM THE PERSIAN EMPIRE
TO ALEXANDER'S DEATH

"Also I in the first year of Darius the Mede, even I, stood to confirm and to strengthen him. *('I stood to confirm and to strengthen him,' refers to Michael the Archangel helping Gabriel as it regards the conflict in question. We see from all this that force has to be used to remove certain satanic rulers [fallen Angels] regarding particular nations, so that another fallen Angel can take their place, even as it was with the Grecian Empire taking over the*

Medo-Persian Empire. All of this happens in the spirit world and is unseen with the natural eye; however, the effects can definitely be felt.

"All of this tells us that there is always conflict in Satan's kingdom, which is here made obvious.)"

THE MIGHTY KING

"And now will I show you the truth. Behold, there shall stand up yet three kings in Persia; and the fourth shall be far richer than they all: and by his strength through his riches he shall stir up all against the realm of Grecia. *(These three Persian kings were Cyrus, Cambyses, and Darius I. The fourth was Xerxes, who fulfilled this Verse according to riches. Actually, there were six Persian kings after the four mentioned in this Verse; however, the conflict against Greece began with Xerxes, who Gabriel said would 'stir up all against the realm of Grecia.')*

"And a mighty king shall stand up, who shall rule with great dominion, and do according to his will. *(This pertains to Alexander the Great, who gained the throne when he was only 19 years old.)*

"And when he shall stand up, his kingdom shall be broken, and shall be divided toward the four winds of heaven; and not to his posterity, nor according to his dominion which he ruled: for his kingdom shall be plucked up, even for others beside those. *('And when he shall stand up,' means when he was at the height of his power, and refers to Alexander the Great. 'His kingdom shall be broken,' has to do with his sudden death at 32 years old, and to the breaking up of the Grecian Empire into four divisions, which were taken over by four of his generals. 'And not to his posterity, nor according to his dominion which he ruled,' speaks of his son, who should have gotten the throne, but did not. It must be remembered that these Prophecies were given by Daniel nearly 200* *years before they actually came to pass)*" **(Dan. 11:1-4).**

THAT WHICH WILL HAPPEN IN THE FUTURE CONCERNING PLANET EARTH

In fact, despite what many say or think, and despite some bad days, very bad days, which are coming shortly ahead, still, the future of this Planet is glorious.

The great Prophet Habakkuk said:

"For the Earth shall be filled with the knowledge of the Glory of the LORD, as the waters cover the sea. *(This Passage is very similar to what Isaiah said in 11:9 of his Book. As the Lord answers Habakkuk, His Statements, although alluding to coming Babylon, rather uses Babylon to symbolize the world as a whole without God. However, the Holy Spirit proclaims: 'For the Earth shall be filled,' not with injustice, murder, greed, avarice, hate, or oppression, but instead 'with the knowledge of the Glory of the LORD.' This will take place in the coming Millennium, beginning immediately after the Second Coming of Christ)*" **(Hab. 2:14).**

Of course, at this time, the Lord Jesus Christ will be reigning Personally from Jerusalem and will, in fact, be the President, so to speak, of the entirety of the Earth. Actually, He is referred to as, *"KING OF KINGS, AND LORD OF LORDS"* (Rev. 19:16).

True, were it not for the Second Coming, man would eventually succeed in destroying himself and, actually, the entirety of the Planet. But, the Lord most definitely will intervene and will do so with Power and Glory such as the world has never previously known.

He came the first time as a lowly Shepherd, so to speak, and was beaten, lampooned, caricatured, and ultimately crucified. When He comes back the second time, which will be without sin unto Salvation, meaning that the sin debt was paid at Calvary and that He is now coming to save the world, it will be with a Power and Glory such as the world has never known before. In other words, He will show the Antichrist and all the world, for that matter, just Who He really is and what He can really do. That's when Israel will accept Him as Saviour, as Lord, and as Messiah. Then they will realize that this One Who has come to their rescue is, in fact, the same One they crucified those long years before.

THE KINGDOM AGE

The Kingdom Age, sometimes called the Millennial Reign, will be 1,000 years in duration (Rev. 20:4). It will be a time of prosperity, peace, freedom, and happiness for the entirety of the world. It will not be a time when a few have everything, and most have nothing. It will be a time of plenty, and more than plenty, for everyone. At that time, there will be no favored nations, and other nations, which are in abject poverty. All will be in abundance. In fact, Isaiah said that:

"The wilderness and the solitary place shall be glad for them; and the desert shall rejoice, and blossom as the rose. *(Chapter 34 of Isaiah, which was the first part of this Prophecy, proclaims the cause of all sorrow, pain, heartache, and destruction, which is sin and man's rebellion against God, which will be destroyed by the Lord Jesus Christ; Chapter 35 of Isaiah, which contains the concluding part of the Prophecy, portrays what God can do in a heart and life that is yielded to Him. As the spiritual renewal takes place in hearts and lives, the material, economic, domestic, and physical renewal will take place over the entirety of the Earth as well.)*"

THE GLORY OF THE LORD

"It shall blossom abundantly, and rejoice even with joy and singing: the glory of Lebanon shall be given unto it, the excellency of Carmel and Sharon, they shall see the Glory of the LORD, and the excellency of our God. *('The Glory of the LORD, and the excellency of our God' is the cause of the 'abundant blossoming' and the 'rejoicing even with joy and singing.')*

"Strengthen you the weak hands, and confirm the feeble knees. *(With these exceeding great and precious Promises, the servants of Truth are commanded to strengthen trembling and apprehensive Believers. With the 'Glory of the LORD' now paramount, even the 'weak' gain 'strength,' and 'feeble knees' are no longer so).*

"Say to them who are of a fearful heart, Be strong, fear not: behold, your God will come with vengeance, even God with a recompence; He will come and save you. *(This Passage expresses again the Doctrine of the Coming of the Lord Jesus Christ. As well, this Verse points to the period predicted in II Pet. 3:10 and Rev. 19:11-21. However, we greatly shortchange the Scriptures if we limit this Passage only to the Second Coming of Christ. Its words are pointed at every Child of God in every period.*

"The sentence, 'He will come and save you,' actually says, 'He will come Himself to save you.' There is One Alone Who can save, and He must do it Himself; to do it, He must 'come' to us.)"

HEALING

"Then the eyes of the blind shall be opened, and the ears of the deaf shall be unstopped. *(Verses 5 and 6 had a fulfillment in the Messiah's First Advent, but their moral and plenary fulfillment belong to His Second and future Advent. Christ did not work miracles in His First Advent as mere wonders, but because it was predicted here that when He came, He would work miracles of this nature; hence, His performing these particular miracles proved Him to be the predicted Messiah. But His rejection postponed to the future the wonders and blessings of this entire Chapter.)*

"**Then shall the lame man leap as an hart, and the tongue of the dumb sing: for in the wilderness shall waters break out, and streams in the desert.** *(The entire complexion of that future Glad Day [the Millennium] will be changed. Sickness and disease will be at an end. 'Then' the 'lame man' will not only be able to walk, but will have such freedom of movement that he will be able to 'leap as an hart.' 'Then' the 'bound tongue' will not only be able to speak, but 'sing,' as well!*

"*However, in the spiritual sense, this has even a greater meaning! Due to the Fall, men have been 'spiritually lame' as well as 'spiritually dumb.' 'Then' all such will 'dance in the Spirit' and 'sing His Praises'!*

"*Due to the Fall, the world is a 'wilderness.' But at that time, the 'waters' and 'streams,' signifying the Holy Spirit, will make the 'desert blossom as the rose')*" **(Isa. 35:1-6).**

NO MORE WAR

Some years ago, I read an article stating that the world was spending three million dollars a minute on weapons of war. That's 180 million dollars an hour, translating into over four billion dollars a day, translating into approximately one and a half trillion dollars a year. Think as to what that could do if it were put to rightful use, which it will be in the coming Kingdom Age.

Concerning Christ and that coming time, Isaiah wrote, "*And He (the Lord Jesus Christ) shall judge among the nations, and shall rebuke many people: and they shall beat their swords into plowshares, and their spears into pruninghooks: nation shall not lift up sword against nation, neither shall they learn war anymore*" (Isa. 2:4).

That means that West Point will go out of business; Sandhurst in England will go out of business; and, St. Cyr in France will shut its doors. These are some of the greatest war colleges in the world, and they will be no more.

CONDITIONS DURING THE MILLENNIUM

Read the following very carefully and feel assured that it's going to come to pass exactly as predicted. The great Prophet said:

"**The wolf also shall dwell with the lamb, and the leopard shall lie down with the kid; and the calf and the young lion and the fatling together; and a little child shall lead them.** *(The character and nature of the Planet, including its occupants and even the animal creation, will revert to their posture as before the Fall.)*

"**And the cow and the bear shall feed** *(feed together)***; their young ones shall lie down together: and the lion shall eat straw like the ox.** *(This Passage plainly tells us that the carnivorous nature of the animal kingdom will be totally and eternally changed.)*

"**And the sucking child shall play on the hole of the asp, and the weaned child shall put his hand on the cockatrice' den.** *(Even though some of the curse will remain on the serpent in the Millennium, in that he continues to writhe in the dust, still, the deadly part will be removed [Gen. 3:14])*" **(Isa. 11:6-8).**

EZEKIEL

The great Prophet Ezekiel tells us in his Book of the building of the Millennial Temple in Jerusalem. He tells us that out from under the threshold, which will be out from under the door leading into the Temple, there will flow a river, with part of it going to the Dead Sea, which will no longer be dead, and part toward the Mediterranean.

On both sides of this river, which will run approximately 60 miles, the Prophet said:

"**And by the River upon the bank thereof, on this side and on that side** *(both sides)***, shall grow all trees for meat, whose leaf shall not fade, neither shall the fruit thereof**

be consumed: it shall bring forth new fruit according to
his months, because their waters they issued out of the
Sanctuary: and the fruit thereof shall be for meat, and
the leaf thereof for medicine. *(Ezekiel is shown the purpose of these miracle trees which grow on either side of
these Rivers. These 'trees' shall perpetually bring forth
new fruit because they are nourished by waters issuing
from the Sanctuary. The fruit will heal as well as nourish.
Such is the character of a Life and Ministry based upon
Calvary and energized by the Holy Spirit.*

*"In fact, the population of the world [which will include
all, with the exception of the Glorified Saints] will continue
to live perpetually by the means of the 'fruit' and the 'leaf'
of these trees. In other words, the aging process at a certain point will be halted. Of course, as it should be understood, Glorified Saints will not need such)"* **(Ezek. 47:12).**

The evidence is that these trees will bear fruit 12 months
out of the year, with that fruit and their leaves transported
all over the world, which will guarantee an abundance for all.
The *"fruit"* and the *"leaves"* will not so much heal sickness as
it will prevent sickness. This means that there really won't be
any sickness in the coming Kingdom Age, neither any poverty,
neither any war, etc. That's when the *"knowledge of the Word
of the Lord shall cover the Earth as the waters cover the sea."*

Of course, after the Kingdom Age will come the eternal
age, which will be without end. At that time, God will transfer
His Headquarters from Planet Heaven, so to speak, down to
Planet Earth, where He will abide with men forever and forever. Chapters 21 and 22 of the great Book of Revelation give
us the information concerning this coming eternal time.

That is the future of Planet Earth, and, to be sure, we have
only scratched the surface. Let me say it again, admittedly,
the world would be completely destroyed were it not for the
Second Coming of our Lord, but, to be sure and to be certain,
He is coming back.

Chapter Two

THE RISE OF THE ANTICHRIST

Many people ask the question, *"Cannot Satan read the Bible, which tells of his utter defeat?"* Of course, he can; however, he is so self-deceived that he does not believe the Bible. Despite Calvary, Satan still believes that he is going to take the day. In fact, his greatest thrust, his greatest effort, is just ahead. He will empower the Antichrist as he has empowered no other man in human history.

This man is referred to in the Bible as *"the Beast"* (Rev. 13:1), *"the Antichrist"* (I Jn. 2:18), *"Gog"* (Ezek. 39:1), *"that Wicked"* (II Thess. 2:8), and *"the man of sin"* (II Thess. 2:3).

WHO WILL HE BE?

As to who he is, the Bible doesn't say.

I think it is obvious, however, that he will have to be a Jew. The Jews would in no way accept a Gentile as their proposed Messiah. They will accept this man, claiming him to be their Messiah, which means that he has to be Jewish. Considering that Jews are scattered all over the world, this means that he could come from any number of places.

The Jews are a peculiar people. Having been out of the Will of God for over 2,000 years, it has taken a deadly toll on them and their nature. In this country of America, some few Jews are conservative, but most are liberal, even extremely liberal.

A PERSONAL EXPERIENCE

If I remember correctly, the year was 1987. I was asked to speak at a Jewish symposium in Washington, D.C. Influential Jews would be present from all over America. Benjamin Netanyahu was the other speaker. He was not Prime Minister of Israel then, such coming a little later.

After the session was over, I had the opportunity to meet the man who is now the Prime Minister of Israel.

I recall almost nothing about the meeting, but I do remember that when I walked away, I sensed in my spirit that this man was going to play a great part in the future of Israel.

At any rate, after the meeting was ended, I had been asked previously to meet with the Jewish liaison to Congress. I spent nearly two hours with the man.

He mentioned to me that he did not understand how that President Reagan, whom most Jews did not support, had turned out to be one of, if not, the greatest friend that the Nation of Israel ever had. Thinking that all conservatives were opposed to Israel, he asked me how this could be.

I explained to him that the Christian movement in America was mostly conservative, but yet, loved Israel very, very much. I went on to tell him how that I personally felt that President Reagan personally had positive feelings toward Israel, but, as well, he was, no doubt, helped along, as it regarded Israel, by the hundreds of thousands of Born-Again Believers in this nation.

So, from that conversation, it is easy for me to see how that Israel can accept a Jew from almost anywhere, considering that he meets with their approval.

There is some Biblical indication that the man of sin will be a Syrian Jew (Dan. 11:40). However, we must understand that the *"king of the north,"* who will be the Antichrist, includes modern Syria, Lebanon, and Iraq. Actually, Iran, Afghanistan, and even some of modern Pakistan, were also included in the old Syrian division of the Grecian Empire. However, some say they are not to be included because they were not a part of the old Roman Empire territory from which the ten horns came up (Dan. 7:7). Possibly, that is true but not necessarily so.

Some claim that the Antichrist will be a reincarnation of Judas, others claim that he will be a reincarnation of Alexander the Great, etc. There is nothing Biblical that supports a reincarnation of anyone.

THE DEBUT OF THE MAN OF SIN

The Antichrist will make his debut, promising great peace, and will be believed by much of the world. Concerning this, the Scripture says:

"**And I saw when the Lamb opened one of the Seals** *(refers to the Crucified, risen Christ, and is proven by the use of the word 'Lamb')*, **and I heard, as it were the noise of thunder, one of the four Beasts** *(living creatures)* **saying, Come and see.** *(This will follow the Rapture of the Church, but we aren't told exactly how long after the Rapture the Great Tribulation will come. 'Come and see,' says that it is destined and cannot be avoided.)*

"**And I saw, and behold a white horse** *(symbolic; proclaims the Antichrist presenting himself to the world as a prince of peace)*: **and he who sat on him had a bow** *(mentions no arrows; he preaches peace, but is preparing for war, as symbolized by the 'bow')*; **and a crown was given unto him: and he went forth conquering, and to conquer.** *(The 'crown' represents the fact that he will conquer many countries. At first, he does so by peace, but will quickly graduate to war)*" **(Rev. 6:1-2).**

THE SEVEN YEAR CONCORD WITH ISRAEL

As we have already stated, Israel, and especially Jerusalem, is the flash point of the world at this time. Surrounded by over 100 million Muslims, who swear her destruction, she occupies a very precarious position. And then, her greatest benefactor of all, the United States, is weakening in its resolve toward her. In fact, the Obama Administration is not only not favorable toward Israel but, if the truth be known, actively opposes her.

Since the Administration of Jimmy Carter, the brightest minds have tried to solve the thorny problem of Israel and the Palestinians. Most of the world thinks that the problem is that Israel will not give land to the Palestinians in order that they might form a nation. Nothing could be further from the truth!

As Arafat once said, *"We will win out over Israel by the means of piece – piece by piece."* The truth is, the Muslim world demands the entirety of the Nation of Israel, with Jerusalem as their capital and the country then named Palestine. As well, they want every Jew dead.

It must be remembered that every war between Israel and the surrounding Arab countries, such as Egypt and Syria, etc., has always been instigated by the Muslims. Israel did not start any of these wars, and yet, they have won every war and then allowed the Palestinians to remain in Israel. If the situation was reversed, and the Muslims had their way, meaning they had won any one of these wars, they would have slaughtered every single Jew. But the world doesn't see that because they don't want to see that. In fact, the world as a whole wouldn't care if Ahmadinejad was able to secure for himself an atomic bomb and then would use it on Israel.

The only friend in the world that Israel has presently is Canada, and what is left of the friendship of America.

So, the brightest minds in America, as already stated, from the time of Jimmy Carter, have tried to solve this thorny problem between Israel and the Palestinians, but with no success. President Bush bragged to the world that before he left office, there would be a peace treaty between Israel and the Palestinians. It did not happen!

Actually, there is no such thing as Palestinians. The name is derived from the ancient Philistines, and, to be sure, there are no Philistines remaining. The people in Israel, who refer to themselves as Palestinians, are actually Jordanians, Syrians, Egyptians, etc.

CLARK CLIFFORD

Some time back, I had the opportunity to hear a most interesting interview with Clark Clifford, who had been an advisor to every democratic president from Harry Truman all the way to Jimmy Carter. Consequently, he had witnessed so much of modern-day history. As far as I know, this was the last interview that he gave before he died.

As the interview began, it was announced by the host that they would discuss this man's life, and considering his experience, it promised to be a very eye-opening interview, which it was. However, despite what the opening remarks were, the entire hour was spent discussing Israel and its becoming a state in 1948.

Mr. Clifford stated how that he was the youngest advisor to President Truman. He went on to state that due to his youthfulness, he had so little place and position that his advice was little sought at that time. While he was present at all the Cabinet meetings, still, it was almost nothing but look and listen.

Mr. Clifford talked about the great struggle in the mind of President Truman as it regarded the formation of the State of Israel. There were arguments about everything. One of the president's closest friends, George Marshall, even suggested that America purchase a small country in Central America and give that to the Jews.

It must be understood that at that particular time, with World War II having just ended, America, plus many other nations, had a guilty conscience as it regarded the Jews. Hitler had slaughtered over six million of these people, and it seems that very little had been done to try to stop the slaughter.

There were others who claimed that wherever a state for these ancient people was made possible, it should be named something other than Israel.

President Truman's closest friend was George Marshall, and Marshall was vehemently opposed to the formation of the State of Israel. So, the argument flew back and forth.

THE LETTER

In answer to the questions posed by the host, Clifford stated that he felt very strongly about Israel becoming a state, how that state must be in the same boundaries as in the Bible, and the state must be named *"Israel."* He was asked why he felt that way; was he Jewish?

"No," he answered, *"I'm not Jewish."* He remarked as to how he did not understand why he felt as he did but in his thinking, he felt he had to somehow get his views to the president. So, he wrote a letter.

He stated that he couldn't get an audience with the president, so, assured that the letter would be delivered to the Oval Office, he put down on paper that which he felt about Israel.

A couple of weeks passed, and he forgot about the letter. Then the President's Secretary called him, stating, *"Mr. Clifford, the president wants to see you. Would you be in his office in the morning at 9 a.m.?"* He asked the Secretary, *"Do you know what the president wants?"*

She answered in the negative.

The next morning, he was there as he had been called.

He stated how that he walked into the Oval Office and stood before the desk of the president. President Truman was looking down at a letter on his desk and after a few moments, Mr. Clifford recognized it as his letter.

President Truman finally looked up to his youthful advisor and stated, *"Clark, why do you feel this strongly about Israel, actually stating that her boundaries must be the Biblical boundaries, and that this new state must be called 'Israel'?"*

The question threw him, he went on to say. He had no time to think up an answer. Why did he feel as strongly as he did?

He finally blurted out, *"Mr. President, I feel as I do because it is the right thing to do."*

He said that the president looked at him for a few moments and then finally said, *"Thank you Clark, that's all!"*

He turned and walked from the room, not really knowing if the president appreciated his answer or not. At any rate, he stated that in a couple of weeks, the president announced to the world that he was going to throw the full weight and prestige of the United States of America behind the formation of a state for the Jews, that it must be in the Biblical boundaries, and that is must be named *"Israel."*

He went on to say that he had no idea if his letter had anything to do with the president's decision, but he did feel that if he had any influence at all on the president, that this was one of the greatest things that he accomplished in his many years of serving as advisor to a number of democratic presidents.

ISRAEL

In fact, shortly before President Truman died, he was taking his customary walk, which he did every morning. That particular morning, a reporter was with him. He was going to write an article on the president, and he was doing all he could to get some information.

He asked the president, *"What do you consider to be the thing that you are most proud of that you were able to accomplish as president?"*

He was speaking with the man who had given the orders to drop two atomic bombs on Japan, which ended World War II. This was the man, as well, who had instigated the Marshall Plan to save Western Europe from Communism.

The President looked at him and said, *"I consider the most*

*important thing that I was able to accomplish while in office was
the part I played in helping Israel to become a Nation."*

The reporter was taken somewhat aback, expecting another
answer.

As stated, this was not long before the president passed
away. Quite possibly, spiritual things were on his mind.
Irrespective, his answer was absolutely correct. He had been
led by the Lord to do what he did, in other words, God used
him to help fulfill Bible Prophecy. Nothing could be more
important than that.

THE BEGINNING OF THE GREAT TRIBULATION

At the moment the Antichrist signs the seven-year agreement between Israel and the Muslim world, the Great
Tribulation begins. As we've already stated, he will be able to
do what the brightest minds in America and elsewhere in the
world have not been able to do—bring together the Israelis
and the Muslims. How will he do that?

As we've also already stated, the man of sin will be anointed
by the powers of darkness as no other human being has ever
been. In other words, Satan will invest more in this man than
he has invested in any other down through the ages. This is
Satan's fell swoop, so to speak. If he doesn't carry out his scheme
now to become master of the Universe, in other words, dethron-
ing God, he will never be able to do it. This is it, the moment
toward which he has worked even from the dawn of time.

To be sure, Satan is self-deceived. He is so deceived that
despite what he knows about God as the Creator and being
all-powerful and all-knowing, still, he actually thinks that he
will be able to overcome the Lord and set his throne up in the
place of God.

SATAN

The great Prophet Isaiah gives us a clue as to the thinking

of the Evil One. Through the Prophet, the Holy Spirit tells us:

"How are you fallen from Heaven, O Lucifer, son of
the morning! how are you cut down to the ground, which
did weaken the nations! *(Isaiah's Prophecy now switches
from the Antichrist to his unholy sponsor, Satan himself.*

*" 'Lucifer' is the name of Satan. Actually, he is an
Angel, originally created by God, who served the Lord in
Righteousness for an undetermined period of time.*

*"When he fell, he led a revolution against God, with
about one-third of the Angels, it seems, throwing in their
lot with him [Rev. 12:4]. Therefore, all the pain, suffering, misery, heartache, death, and deception, which have
ruled the nations from the very beginning, can be laid at
the doorstep of this revolution headed up by Satan.)*"

I WILL BE LIKE GOD?

"For you have said in your heart, I will ascend into
Heaven, I will exalt my throne above the stars of God:
I will sit also upon the mount of the congregation, in the
sides of the north:

"I will ascend above the heights of the clouds; I will
be like the Most High. *(In these two Verses, we see the
foment of Satan's rebellion and revolution against God.
It seems that Lucifer, while true to the Lord, was given
dominion of the Earth, which was before Adam. After his
fall, he worked deceitfully to get other angelic rulers to
follow him in his war against God.)*

"Yet you shall be brought down to Hell, to the sides
of the pit. *(This would be the lot of Satan and all who seek
to be like God, but in a wrong way, in effect, by making
themselves god)*" (Isa. 14:12-15).

The Evil One has deceived himself in the same manner that
he has deceived much of the world and for all time. However,

the conclusion for him, and for all who have followed him, and who do follow him, will be eternal Hell, i.e., *"the Lake of Fire"* (Rev. 20:10).

A WEEK OF YEARS

How is it that we know this agreement, which will be signed by the Antichrist, plus Israel and the Muslims, and, no doubt, others, as well, will last for seven years?

Daniel is the Prophet who gave this information and did so about 2,500 years ago. The account is found in the Ninth Chapter of the Book of Daniel.

The great Prophet, it seems, had been in prayer before the Lord for a period of time. At a given point, the Angel Gabriel appeared to him. I will quote verbatim from THE EXPOSITOR'S STUDY BIBLE.

GABRIEL

"And while I was speaking, and praying, and confessing my sin and the sin of my people Israel, and presenting my supplication before the LORD my God for the Holy Mountain of my God *(Daniel declared that Jerusalem has been called by God's Name and has been chosen by God. Actually, it will be the capital of His Eternal Kingdom on Earth [Ps. 2:6; 48:2; 87:2; 102:16; 132:13; Isa. 2:2-4; Ezek., Chpt. 48; Zech., Chpt. 14])*;

"Yes, while I was speaking in prayer, even the man Gabriel, whom I had seen in the Vision at the beginning, being caused to fly swiftly, touched me about the time of the evening oblation. *(Once again, 'Gabriel' is sent to Daniel's side. The phrase, 'About the time of the evening oblation,' referred to 3 p.m., which was the time of the evening sacrifice; however, this does not imply that those offerings were made in Babylon, but simply that, through the nearly seventy years that had intervened since the fall of Jerusalem, the sacred hour had been kept in remembrance, and possibly as one consecrated to prayer.)*"

UNDERSTANDING

"**And he informed me, and talked with me, and said, O Daniel, I am now come forth to give you skill and understanding.** *('To give you skill and understanding,' refers to the future of Israel and last-day events.)*

"**At the beginning of your supplications the Commandment came forth, and I am come to show you; for you are greatly beloved: therefore understand the matter, and consider the Vision.** *(The study of Bible Prophecy was not for Daniel a mere intellectual entertainment but moral and Spiritual Nourishment.)*"

SEVENTY WEEKS OF YEARS

"**Seventy weeks are determined upon your people** *(Israel)* **and upon your holy city** *(Jerusalem)*, **to finish the transgression, and to make an end of sins, and to make reconciliation for iniquity, and to bring in everlasting Righteousness, and to seal up the Vision and Prophecy, and to anoint the Most Holy.** *('Seventy weeks are determined upon your people,' actually means seventy sevens, which translates into 490 years. This period of time has to do with 'your people' and 'your holy city,' referring to the Jews and Jerusalem. The Second Coming of Christ and their acceptance of Him will 'finish the transgression.'*

"*'To make reconciliation [atonement] for iniquity,' refers to the fact that Israel will not only accept Christ at the Second Coming but will also accept what He did for us at Calvary. One can well imagine this moment, for they are the ones who crucified Christ.*

"*The phrase, 'To anoint the Most Holy,' has to do with the building of the Millennial Temple, even as described by*

Ezekiel in Chapters 40 through 48 of his Book.)"

TROUBLOUS TIMES

"Know therefore and understand, that from the going forth of the Commandment to restore and to build Jerusalem unto the Messiah the Prince shall be seven weeks, and threescore and two weeks: the street shall be built again, and the wall, even in troublous times. *(If one is to notice in this Scripture, the 'seventy weeks of years' is broken up into two periods. One 'shall be seven weeks' [49 years] and the other will be 'threescore and two weeks [434 years], totaling 483 years. 'That from the going forth of the Commandment to restore and rebuild Jerusalem,' is the beginning of this 490-year period. However, from that time until it was actually finished was some 141 years. Actually, the clock stopped and started several times, so to speak, in this 141-year period, totaling some 49 years when work was truly in progress, comprising the first seven weeks of years [49 years]. In other words, it took 141 years for Jerusalem to be rebuilt after its destruction by Nebuchadnezzar, but work was in progress only 49 years in that period of time. So, as we have stated, the clock stopped and started several times during that period.*

"The second block of time started at the end of the 49 years and ended with the Crucifixion of the Lord Jesus Christ, which was 434 years. Combining, as stated, the 49 years with the 434 years brings the total to 483 years.

"The third block of time, which we will study in the last Verse, will be the last week of years, totaling seven years, which will make up the Great Tribulation period, concluding Daniel's Prophecy of seventy weeks of years.

"Again, it must be remembered that these 490 years did not run consecutively. There were stoppages, as stated, in the first 49 years; then there has been a huge halt of nearly 2,000 years from the time that Christ was crucified,

which has not concluded yet. In other words, the last week of years [seven years] is yet to come and will comprise the time frame of the Great Tribulation.)"

THE CRUCIFIXION OF CHRIST

"And after threescore and two weeks shall Messiah be cut off, but not for Himself: and the people of the prince who shall come shall destroy the city and the Sanctuary; and the end thereof shall be with a flood, and unto the end of the war desolations are determined. *(The phrase, 'And after threescore and two weeks shall Messiah be cut off,' gives us the exact time, even the very year, that the Messiah would be crucified. The words, 'cut off,' refer to His Crucifixion.*

"'But not for Himself,' refers to Jesus dying for mankind and taking upon Himself the penalty for mankind. In other words, He did not die for crimes he had committed, but rather for the crimes mankind had committed.

"'And the people of the prince who shall come shall destroy the city and the Sanctuary,' refers to the Romans, who fulfilled this Prophecy in A.D. 70. However, the 'prince,' as used here, actually refers to the Antichrist, who has not yet come but will come from among the ten kingdoms yet to be formed inside the old Roman Empire territory. The next Verse proves this.)"

SEVEN YEARS

"And he shall confirm the covenant with many for one week: and in the midst of the week he shall cause the sacrifice and the oblation to cease, and for the overspreading of abominations he shall make it desolate, even until the consummation, and that determined shall be poured upon the desolate. *('And he shall confirm,' refers to the Antichrist. The phrase, 'And in the midst of the week,' refers to three and a half years, at which time the Antichrist will show his true colors and stop the sacrifices in the newly-built Temple. At that time, he will actually invade Israel, with her suffering her first military defeat since her formation as a Nation in 1948.*

" 'Even until the consummation,' means until the end of the seven-year Great Tribulation period. The phrase, 'And that determined shall be poured upon the desolate,' refers to all the Prophecies being fulfilled regarding the great suffering that Israel will go through the last three and a half years of the Great Tribulation [Mat. 24:21-22])" (Dan. 9:20-27).

WILL THE ANTICHRIST KNOW THAT HE IS FULFILLING BIBLE PROPHECY BY SIGNING THIS SEVEN-YEAR AGREEMENT?

I doubt seriously that he will know such! Unredeemed people don't care very much for the Bible, and even if they do read it, they understand little of what they read.

We have stated at times that the Bible is really not easy to understand. It is made up of about one-third history, one-third Prophecy, and one-third instruction. The information we have just given concerning Daniel concerns Prophecy. Were it not for the notes from THE EXPOSITOR'S STUDY BIBLE that we have given concerning the interpretation of these Passages in this Ninth Chapter of Daniel, to be frank, most Christians would not understand it.

HOW WILL THE ANTICHRIST BE ABLE TO BROKER AN AGREEMENT BETWEEN ISRAEL AND THE MUSLIMS WHEN EVERYONE ELSE HAS FAILED?

As we've already stated, he will be anointed by the powers of darkness more so than any other man who's ever lived. In other words, to use some street terminology, Satan is putting his money altogether on this *"man of sin."*

What I'm about to give, as it regards this thorny question, is not found in the Bible. Neither am I saying that the Lord gave it to me. He might have, but everything that comes to my mind is not necessarily given by the Lord. So, I would rather err on the side of caution if forced to err at all.

I would ask you to read the following very carefully, which could very well portray the means and the ways that this deal will be brokered.

Please understand, when these agreements are signed, the Antichrist will be the topic of conversation on every television talk show, every radio talk show, the headline of every news-paper, and the topic of subject in every major magazine in the world. In other words, he is going to be the golden boy of the time. In fact, at that time, Israel will declare to the whole world that this one is actually her Messiah. There is a possibility that even the Muslims, who, incidentally, are looking for a Messiah, could declare the same thing. But yet, this doesn't answer the question as to how he will be able to broker this deal. The following just might be the way that it will be carried out:

THE HEIGHT OF DECEPTION

We do know that Israel is going to build her Temple and will actually begin offering up sacrifices. I wonder what the animal rights people will say to that.

There is argument among Bible scholars presently as to exactly where this Temple will be built.

Some have claimed that it could be built beside the Dome of the Rock, which is the so-called third most holy place in the world of Islam. They claim that Muhammad went to Heaven on a winged horse from this very spot. Actually, there is no proof that Muhammad was ever in Jerusalem, but, be that as it may, this is still a very revered spot for the Muslims. I cannot conceive of the Muslims allowing the Jewish Temple to be built on the Temple Mount close by the Dome of the Rock. As well,

I cannot see Israel allowing the Dome of the Rock, which they consider to be heathenistic, to be close to their Temple.

Others have suggested that the Great Synagogue in Jerusalem could be used in the place of the Temple.

I cannot see Israel putting her Temple any place other than the exact spot where Solomon's Temple once sat, which is where God originally stated that it should be.

If one would walk inside the Dome of the Rock, he would see a circular fence around a rock protrusion. It is claimed that at this exact spot is where Abraham was to offer Isaac, in other words, that an altar was built on top of that rock. Of course, all students of the Bible know that God stopped Abraham at the last moment. In fact, it is also believed that the Holy of Holies in Solomon's Temple sat over this exact spot—the rock where Isaac was to be offered. So, this spot is more sacred to Israel than anything else.

The Lord told David to build the Temple in the exact spot where he offered up sacrifices to stop the plague from destroying Jerusalem (II Sam. 24:18-25). The Scripture says:

> "Then Solomon began to build the House of the LORD at Jerusalem in Mount Moriah *(this is the first mention of Mount Moriah since Gen. 22:2; it is never mentioned after this; it is where Abraham was to offer up Isaac)*, where the LORD appeared unto David his father, in the place that David had prepared in the threshingfloor of Ornan *(Araunah)* the Jebusite *(a place of Judgment, the destroying Angel [II Sam. 24:16], now turned into a place of Blessing, all by the Grace of God)*.
>
> "And he began to build in the second day of the second month, in the fourth year of his reign" (II Chron. 3:1-2).

Actually, it is said that if the Temple was built presently and done in the exact manner that it was built then, with the same materials being used, it would cost over 10 billion dollars. This was the only building in the world where God dwelt, and He did so in the Holy of Holies, between the Mercy Seat and the Cherubim.

When Nebuchadnezzar destroyed Solomon's Temple, a crude structure was ultimately built by Zerubbabel in its place. This was when Israel was allowed to leave the Medo-Persian Empire and come back and rebuild their city and temple, etc. Then, a few years before Christ, on the exact same spot, Herod built one of the most beautiful buildings in the world. This is the one that Jesus said to His Disciples, *"Do you not see all these things? verily I say unto you, There shall not be left here one stone upon another, that shall not be thrown down"* (Mat. 24:2). And that's exactly what happened.

VESPASIAN

Vespasian commanded the mighty Roman Tenth Legion, which laid siege to Judaea, and then to Jerusalem. It was probably the greatest field army in the world at that time.

Caesar died and Vespasian was called to Rome where he became Caesar. His son Titus took his place as head of the Tenth Legion.

Titus gave instructions that the Temple was to be spared, in that it was one of the most beautiful structures in the world. However, his soldiers did not respect him as they had respected his father. They had heard that there was gold in the mortar between the huge stones, and, ignoring the command that he had given for the Temple to be spared, they literally pulled down the Temple, stone by stone, actually hooking oxen to the great stones and toppling them. Incidentally, they found no gold in the mortar.

They even plowed the ground where the Temple had sat, fulfilling the Prophecy of our Lord in totality. So, Israel now, and I speak of this present time (2011), wants to build her Temple and once again institute the sacrifices. I cannot see them building this Temple in any place except where Solomon's Temple had sat, etc., but to build it there, the Dome of the Rock is going to have to be torn down. How in the world will the Antichrist be able to convince the Muslim leaders to allow Israel to tear down the Dome of the Rock?

That's the question!

THE GREAT DECEPTION

It is possible that the Antichrist will call together the leading Muslim clerics in the world, with the following intention in mind:

He will require of them to go along with him regarding his proposal. It is to grant Israel her borders, which she has requested, whatever that will be at the time. And then, he will present the greatest problem of all, that they agree to allow Israel to tear down the Dome of the Rock, so they can build their Temple. To be sure, the Muslims are going to swallow hard on that request.

I believe that he will succeed in getting them to agree to what he is saying.

How?

He could tell them, *"Go along with me on these things. Allow Israel to have the borders she so desires and allow Israel to build her Temple, even though it will mean you having to tear down the Dome of the Rock. If you do this,"* he will promise, *"when my strength is sufficient, and it will be shortly, I will then turn on Israel, attack her with all of my power, and completely destroy her. Then you can have the entirety of the State of Israel and name it whatever you desire, plus tear down her Temple and rebuild your Dome."*

It should be understood that the Muslims are allowed by the Koran to lie if it will help Islam. So, the truth is, you can't really depend on anything they say. At any rate, the world will not know of this backroom deal and will herald the Antichrist as the man who has brought peace to the world. In other words, he has put out the flickering flame that could explode into a conflagration at any time.

At the moment the papers are signed, as stated, the seven-year Great Tribulation begins.

THE FALSE MESSIAH

Israel, at that time, will be so enamored with this man, believing that he has secured her future, that she will automatically declare him as the Messiah. This is what Jesus was talking about when He said:

"I am come in My Father's Name, and you receive Me not: if another shall come in his own name, him you will receive" (Jn. 5:43). The *"another,"* to whom He alluded, is the Antichrist.

THE *"LITTLE HORN"*: ANTICHRIST

The Word of God has much to say about this *"man of sin,"* who is soon to come, and will turn the world to sin and shame as it has never known before. In fact, he will endeavor to take over the entirety of the Planet. He would succeed but for the Second Coming of the Lord.

Without a doubt, the great Prophet Daniel had more to say about this coming man of sin than anyone else in the Word of God. He said, and we quote directly from THE EXPOSITOR'S STUDY BIBLE:

"I considered the horns, and, behold, there came up among them another little horn, before whom there were three of the first horns plucked up by the roots: and, behold, in this horn were eyes like the eyes of a man, and a mouth speaking great things. *(At first, Daniel did not understand the horns. Even though the Roman Empire has come and gone, still, the 'ten horns' have not yet risen to power; however, the breakup of the former Soviet Union is the beginning of the fulfillment of this Passage. If one is to notice, the 'ten horns' were a part of the non-descript beast [described in Dan. 7:7], which has to do with the territory which the old Roman Empire controlled.*

" 'There came up among them another little horn, 'means this one came up after the 'ten horns' were fully grown. The 'little horn' is the Antichrist.

"Three of the horns will be plucked by the 'little horn,' meaning that he will defeat these countries in battle, with the others then submitting to him. This will take place in the first half of the Great Tribulation)" **(Dan. 7:8).**

A MOUTH THAT SPOKE VERY GREAT THINGS

Daniel continues:

"And of the ten horns that were in his head, and of the other which came up, and before whom three fell; even of that horn that had eyes, and a mouth that spoke very great things, whose look was more stout than his fellows. *(The 'other which came up' is the same as the 'little horn' of Verse 8 and is the Antichrist, who will come on the world scene shortly after the Rapture of the Church [II Thess. 2:7-8].)*

"I beheld, and the same horn made war with the Saints, and prevailed against them *(the 'Saints' mentioned here are not the Church, but rather Israel. The 'war' spoken of here concerns the Antichrist signing a seven-year non-aggression pact with Israel and then breaking it at approximately the midpoint, then declaring war on Israel)"* **(Dan. 7:20-21).**

A TIME AND TIMES AND THE DIVIDING OF TIME

"And he shall speak great words against the Most High, and shall wear out the Saints of the Most High, and think to change times and laws: and they shall be given into his hand until a time and times and the dividing of time. *('And he shall speak great words against the*

Most High,' is used several times by the Holy Spirit in various ways, drawing our attention to the blasphemy of the Antichrist.

"The phrase, 'And they shall be given into his hand until a time and times and the dividing of time,' refers to Israel being defeated and being greatly persecuted for a period of three and a half years)" **(Dan. 7:25).**

THE ANTICHRIST

Daniel continues to give more information:

"And out of one of them came forth a little horn, which waxed exceeding great, toward the south, and toward the east, and toward the pleasant land. *('And out of one of them came forth a little horn,' refers to the future Antichrist coming out of one of these four divisions of the old Grecian Empire. 'Toward the south' refers to Egypt; 'toward the east' refers to Syria, Iraq, and Iran; 'toward the pleasant land' refers to Israel. From this area, the Antichrist will make his bid for world dominion.)"*

THE ANTICHRIST BREAKS HIS SEVEN-YEAR COVENANT WITH ISRAEL

"And it waxed great, even to the host of heaven; and it cast down some of the host and of the stars to the ground, and stamped upon them. *('And it waxed great, even to the host of heaven,' refers to the 'little horn' [Antichrist] breaking his seven-year covenant with Israel, which Daniel speaks of in a future Vision [Dan. 9:27], actually declaring war on Israel at that time, seeking to destroy her. This is symbolized by the phrase, 'And it [little horn] cast down some of the host and of the stars to the ground, and stamped upon them,' referring to Israel being defeated at that time, which is yet future.)"*

THE DAILY SACRIFICES STOPPED

"Yes, he magnified himself even to the prince of the host, and by him the daily sacrifice was taken away, and the place of his sanctuary was cast down. *('Yes, he magnified himself even to the prince of the host,' refers to the Antichrist usurping authority over the High Priest of Israel. These Verses actually speak of the war, which will be instituted by the Antichrist when he breaks his seven-year covenant with Israel and other countries, actually invading the 'pleasant land.' He will defeat Israel and stop the daily sacrifices, which will have been reinstituted by Israel after a lapse of approximately 2,000 years. This tells us that the Jewish Temple is going to be rebuilt.)*"

THE WORLD'S APPLAUSE

"And an host was given him against the daily sacrifice by reason of transgression, and it cast down the truth to the ground; and it practiced, and prospered. *('By reason of transgression,' refers to the Antichrist breaking his seven-year covenant with Israel, therefore, committing 'transgression.' As stated, he will then stop the 'daily sacrifice.' 'And it practiced, and prospered,' refers to the fact that much of the world will applaud him in these actions)*" (Dan. 8:9-12).

TRODDEN UNDERFOOT

"Then I heard one Saint speaking, and another Saint said unto that certain Saint which spoke, How long shall be the Vision concerning the daily sacrifice, and the transgression of desolation, to give both the Sanctuary and the host to be trodden underfoot? *(These are 'Saints' in Heaven; Daniel overheard their conversation but had no identification as to who they were. The 'Sanctuary' spoken of here is the rebuilt Temple in Jerusalem. The 'Host to be trodden underfoot,' refers to the worshippers, with their worship stopped, as well as the High Priest and associating Priests abruptly stopping their duties, if not being killed. This is when the Antichrist invades Israel in the middle of the seven-year tribulation period)"* **(Dan. 8:13).**

THE LITTLE HORN

Daniel now deals with the personality of the man of sin. He said:

"And in the latter time of their kingdom, when the transgressors are come to the full, a king of fierce countenance, and understanding dark sentences, shall stand up. *('And in the latter time of their kingdom,' pertains to the coming of the Antichrist. 'When the transgressors are come to the full,' refers to the Nation of Israel reaching the climax of her guilt by accepting the Antichrist instead of Christ, as predicted by the Lord Himself [Jn. 5:43]. 'A king of fierce countenance, and understanding dark sentences, shall stand up,' proclaims the Antichrist having a majestic presence and superhuman knowledge, which is actually inspired of Satan.)"*

WAR ON ISRAEL

"And his power shall be mighty, but not by his own power: and he shall destroy wonderfully, and shall prosper, and practice, and shall destroy the mighty and the holy People. *('And he shall destroy wonderfully,' refers to Rev. 6:4-8. 'And shall prosper, and practice,' means that his efforts will be extremely successful. 'And shall destroy the mighty and the holy People,' refers to Israel.)"*

HIS WAR WITH THE MESSIAH

"And through his policy also he shall cause craft to

prosper in his hand; and he shall magnify himself in his heart, and by peace shall destroy many: he shall also stand up against the Prince of princes; but he shall be broken without hand. *(The word 'craft' in the Hebrew is 'mirmah,' meaning 'deceit.' The Antichrist will be the greatest deceiver of all [II Thess. 2:8-12; Rev. 13:14; 19:20]. The last phrase, 'He shall stand up against the Prince of princes,' refers to his war against Christ, which will culminate with the Battle of Armageddon [Joel, Chpt. 3; Zech., Chpt. 14; Rev. 16:13-16; 19:11-21])"* **(Dan. 8:23-25).**

We are reading something in the Book of Daniel, giving us information concerning the man of sin, who very well may be alive at this moment but has not been revealed. He will not be revealed until after the Rapture of the Church. When we realize that these Prophecies were given approximately 2,500 years ago, and that they are now beginning to come to pass, it lets us know how great and wonderful the Lord actually is, Who gave Daniel all of this information.

THE ACCOUNT OF THE ENDTIME

"And some of them of understanding shall fall, to try them, and to purge, and to make them white, even to the time of the end: because it is yet for a time appointed. *(With this Verse begins the account of the Endtime, which will continue through the Twelfth Chapter. Therefore, the entirety of the time, now totaling nearly 2,000 years, is omitted in Scripture, which includes the entirety of the Church Age, because Gabriel told Daniel, 'These Prophecies' only pertain to 'your people,' and more particularly, 'in the latter days' [Dan. 10:14].)"*

THE INDIGNATION

"And the king shall do according to his will; and he

shall exalt himself, and magnify himself above every god, and shall speak marvelous things against the God of gods, and shall prosper till the indignation be accomplished: for that that is determined shall be done. *('And the king shall do according to his will,' refers to the Antichrist, who will pretty much have his way until the Second Advent of Christ. 'And magnify himself above every god,' actually refers to him deifying himself [II Thess. 2:4]. At this time, and according to Dan. 9:27, he will take over the newly-built Temple in Jerusalem, do away with the Jewish sacrifices, which have not long since begun, and will set up an image of himself [Rev. 13:15].*

" 'And shall speak marvelous things against the God of gods,' means that he will literally declare war on Christ. His campaign of declaring himself 'god' will, of necessity, demand that he blaspheme the True God as no one has ever blasphemed.

" 'And shall prosper till the indignation be accomplished,' means that much of the world will accept his claims, joining with him in their hatred of the God of the Bible.)"

HE SHALL MAGNIFY HIMSELF

"Neither shall he regard the God of his fathers, nor the desire of women, nor regard any god: for he shall magnify himself above all. *('Neither shall he regard the God of his fathers,' no doubt, refers to him being a Jew. He will not regard the God of 'Abraham, Isaac, and Jacob.'*

" 'Nor the desire of women,' probably refers to him turning against the Catholic church and, thereby, the Virgin Mary, or it could mean that he is a homosexual.

" 'Nor regard any god: for he shall magnify himself above all,' refers to all the religions of the world, all of which will be outlawed, at least, where he has control, demanding that worship be centered upon him.)"

THE GOD OF FORCES

"But in his estate shall he honour the god of forces; and a god whom his fathers knew not shall he honour with gold, and silver, and with precious stones, and pleasant things. *('And a god whom his fathers knew not shall he honour,' refers to a 'strange god' mentioned in the next Verse, who is actually the fallen Angel who empowered Alexander the Great. He is called 'the Prince of Grecia,' which does not refer to a mortal, but instead, a fallen Angel [Dan. 10:20]. This 'god,' his fathers, Abraham, Isaac, and Jacob, did not know.)*"

A STRANGE GOD

"Thus shall he do in the most strong holds with a strange god, whom he shall acknowledge and increase with glory: and he shall cause them to rule over many, and shall divide the land for gain. *('Thus shall he do in the most strong holds,' refers to the great financial centers of the world, which will be characterized by rebuilt Babylon. This 'strange god,' as stated, is a fallen Angel; therefore, he will probably think he is giving praise and glory to himself, when in reality he is actually honoring this 'fallen Angel.'*

"'And he shall cause them to rule over many,' refers to the many nations he will conquer because of the great power given to him by this fallen Angel, instigated by Satan)" (Dan. 11:35-39).

THE KING OF THE NORTH

"And at the time of the end shall the king of the south *(Egypt)* push at him: and the king of the north *(the Antichrist, Syria)* shall come against him like a whirlwind, with chariots, and with horsemen, and with many ships; and he

shall enter into the countries, and shall overflow and pass over. *(The phrase, 'And at the time of the end,' refers to the time of the fulfillment of these Prophecies, which, in fact, is just ahead. It is known that 'the king of the south' refers to Egypt because that's who is referred to at the beginning of this Chapter, which spoke of the breakup of the Grecian Empire. As well, 'the king of the north' proves that the Antichrist will come from the Syrian division of the breakup of the Grecian Empire. So, the Antichrist will more than likely be a Syrian Jew. But we must remember, the Syria of that day included modern Lebanon, Iraq, Iran, and Afghanistan. So, he could come from any one of these countries)"* **(Dan. 11:40).**

ISRAEL

"He shall enter also into the glorious land *(into Israel)*, **and many countries shall be overthrown** *(those in the Middle East)*: **but these shall escape out of his hand, even Edom, and Moab, and the chief of the children of Ammon.** *(Edom, Moab, and Ammon comprise modern Jordan. His entering into the 'glorious land' refers to his invasion of Israel at the midpoint of his seven-year nonaggression pact with them, therefore, breaking his covenant [Dan. 9:27].*

"The countries listed comprise modern Jordan, where ancient Petra is located, to which Israel will flee upon the Antichrist 'entering into the Glorious Land' [Rev. 12:6])" **(Dan. 11:41).**

POWER

"He shall stretch forth his hand also upon the countries: and the land of Egypt shall not escape. *('Egypt' refers to 'the king of the south' of Verse 40, as stated.)*

"But he shall have power over the treasures of gold

and of silver, and over all the precious things of Egypt:
and the Libyans and the Ethiopians shall be at his steps.
*(The 'precious things of Egypt', no doubt, refer to the
ancient mysteries of Egypt, regarding the tombs, the pyra-
mids, etc. He will, no doubt, claim to unlock many of these
mysteries; he very well could do so, regarding the supernatural power given to him by the powers of darkness)*"
(Dan. 11:42-43).

THE MARK OF THE BEAST

John the Beloved, as is obvious, had much to say about the
Antichrist in the Book of Revelation. Please note the following:

"And he caused all, both small and great, rich and
poor, free and bond, to receive a mark in their right
hand, or in their foreheads *('all' represents only those in
his domain, not the entirety of the world; this domain will
include virtually the entirety of the area of the old Roman
Empire, which includes North Africa, the Middle East, and
most of modern Europe; this will be a literal mark)*:
"And that no man might buy or sell, save he who had
the mark *(we are told in Verses 11 through 13 of this Chapter that the seduction of the Antichrist will be religious;
now we are told in Verses 16 and 17 it will be economic)*,
or the name of the beast, or the number of his name.
*(The thought is that either the 'name' of the beast or his
'number' will be required as a brand or mark upon all. As
well, the name could be 'God.')*
"Here is wisdom *(this is the Wisdom of God)*. Let him
who has understanding count the number of the beast
*(the idea is that it is the number of a man, not of God,
which means he will give account to Jehovah, Whom he
has repeatedly blasphemed)*: for it is the number of a
man; and his number *is* Six hundred threescore *and* six.
(It is the number of a man, not a kingdom, not a religion,

not a dispensation, but a man. The number will be 666)"
(Rev. 13:16-18).

THE APOSTLE PAUL

To address some errors that were beginning to circulate
in the Early Church, and especially concerning the Endtime,
Paul gives us the following as it regards Endtime events, which
include the rise of the Antichrist. He said:

"**Let no man deceive you by any means** *(in other
words, don't listen to that which is Scripturally incorrect)*:
for *that day shall not come,* **except there come a falling away first** *(should have been translated, 'for that day
shall not come, except there come a departure first'; this
speaks of the Rapture, which, in essence, says the Second
Coming cannot take place until certain things happen; as
well, and most definitely, apostasy will prevail, also, which
it now does)*, **and that man of sin be revealed, the son of
perdition** *(this speaks of the Antichrist, who must come
upon the world scene before the Second Coming)*;
"**Who opposes and exalts himself above all that
is called God** *(pertains to his declaration of himself as
Deity)*, **or that is worshipped** *(the Antichrist will put down
all religions, at least in the area which he controls, making
himself alone the object of worship)*; **so that he as God
sits in the Temple of God** *(refers to the Jewish Temple,
which will be rebuilt in Jerusalem; the Antichrist will take
over the Temple, making it his religious headquarters)*,
showing himself that he is God. *(This proclaims his
announcement of Deity as it regards Himself.)*"

THE REVEALING OF THE ANTICHRIST

"**Don't you remember, that, when I was yet with
you, I told you these things?** *(So, there was no excuse for*

the Thessalonians to be drawn away by false doctrine.)

"And now you know what withholds *(speaks of the Church)* **that he might be revealed in his time.** *(This speaks of the Antichrist who will be revealed or made known after the Rapture of the Church.)*

"For the mystery of iniquity does already work *(presents false teaching by false teachers)***: only he** *(the Church)* **who now lets** *(who now hinders evil)* ***will let*** *(will continue to hinder)***, until he** *(the Church)* **be taken out of the way.** *(The pronoun 'he' confuses some people. In Verses 4 and 6, the pronoun 'he' refers to the Antichrist, while in Verse 7, 'he' refers to the Church.)*

"And then *(after the Rapture of the Church)* **shall that Wicked** *(the Antichrist)* **be revealed** *(proving conclusively that the Rapture takes place before the Great Tribulation [Mat. 24:21])***, whom the Lord shall consume with the spirit of His Mouth** *(should have been translated, 'the Breath of His Mouth' [Isa. 11:4])***, and shall destroy with the brightness of His Coming** *(both phrases refer to the Second Coming)***" (II Thess. 2:3-8).**

BELIEVING A LIE

"*Even him* (the Antichrist), whose coming is after the working of Satan *(means that Satan is the sponsor of the Antichrist)* **with all power and signs and lying wonders** *(proclaims the fact that the Antichrist's rise to power, at least in the beginning, will be very religious)***,**

"And with all deceivableness of unrighteousness in them who perish *(refers to the fact that 'all lying powers and lying signs and lying wonders' will be used to deceive the world)***; because they received not the love of the Truth, that they might be saved** *(they rejected Christ and the Cross)***.**

"And for this cause *(the rejection of Christ and the Cross)* **God shall send them strong delusion** *(if one doesn't* *want 'the Truth,' God will see to it one receives a 'delusion'),* **that they should believe a lie** *(should have been translated, 'that they should believe the lie'; the Greek Text has the definite article 'the lie,' which refers to a specific lie; that 'lie' pertains to anything that leads a person away from the Cross)***:**

"That they all might be damned who believed not the Truth *(who would not accept the Cross)***, but had pleasure in unrighteousness.** *(The Greek has the definite article, which actually says, 'the unrighteousness,' specifying a particular unrighteousness; it is really referring to the results of rejection of the Cross of Christ)***" (II Thess. 2:9-12).**

CHAPTER THREE

THE HATRED OF ISRAEL

- There is an animosity against Jews all over the world. Why?
- There is an animosity against those who are truly Believers in Christ. Why?
- There is a hatred of Jesus Christ all over the world. Why?

Let's look at the origin of this hatred before we deal with the *"why"* of this hatred.

Immediately after the Fall in the Garden of Eden, the Lord addressed Satan through the serpent. As is obvious in the Genesis account, the serpent had lent its body and faculties, such as they were, to Satan, which pertained to the temptation of Eve. The Scripture says concerning this:

> "And the LORD God said unto the serpent *(as we shall see, presents no question or interrogation being posed toward the serpent at all; God judges him, and it is in listening to this judgment that the guilty pair hear the first great Promise respecting Christ)*, Because you have done this, you are cursed above all cattle, and above every beast of the field *(refers to this animal being reduced from*

possibly the highest place and position in the animal king-dom to the lowest); **upon your belly shall you go, and dust shall you eat all the days of your life** *(if, in fact, the serpent was an unwitting tool in the hand of Satan, then I think that the Lord would not have placed a curse upon this animal)*" **(Gen. 3:14).**

And now we come to the part that tells us the *"why"* of this animosity between mankind in general and the Lord Jesus Christ. The Lord said to Satan:

"And I will put enmity *(animosity)* **between you and the woman** *(presents the Lord now actually speaking to Satan, who had used the serpent; in effect, the Lord is saying to Satan, 'You used the woman to bring down the human race, and I will use the woman as an instrument to bring the Redeemer into the world, Who will save the human race')*, **and between your seed** *(mankind which follows Satan)* **and her Seed** *(the Lord Jesus Christ)*; **it** *(Christ)* **shall bruise your head** *(the Victory that Jesus won at the Cross [Col. 2:14-15])*, **and you shall bruise His Heel** *(the sufferings of the Cross)*" **(Gen. 3:15).**

THE CAUSE FOR THE ANIMOSITY

The reason for the animosity against the Lord Jesus Christ and all who follow Him is that Jesus Christ is real, whereas all the other claimed deities are just figments of man's imagination. In other words, there is no such thing as *"Allah."* In fact, the name *"Allah"* was one of the Babylonian deities of old, which was selected by Muhammad, etc. The real truth is, *"Allah"* is a demon spirit, the same as all other supposed deities, other than the Lord Jesus Christ.

There is only one God but manifested in Three Persons. Those Three are, *"God the Father, God the Son, and God the Holy Spirit."*

The name or title *"God"* does not garner much animosity because the name or title *"God"* is almost a generic term. In other words, many things are referred to as God, so that part of the world, which is almost all who don't serve the Lord Jesus Christ, takes very little offense, if any at all, at the name *"God."* However, Jesus Christ is something else altogether.

The reason for that is very simple as well.

Jesus said:

"... I am the Way, the Truth, and the Life *(proclaims in no uncertain terms exactly Who and What Jesus is)*: no man comes unto the Father, but by Me *(He declares positively that this idea of God as Father, this approach to God for every man, is through Him – through what He is and what He has done, referring to the Cross)*" **(Jn. 14:6).**

It is ironic, the Jews hate Jesus Christ, and the world that does not care for Jesus Christ either, hates the Jews because they killed Christ. It is somewhat like the old proverb of *"the pot calling the kettle black."*

However, the real reason for the animosity of the world against the Jews is simply because of their past and what will transpire in their future.

Jesus said to the woman of Samaria, *"... Salvation is of the Jews"* (Jn. 4:22).

What did He mean by that?

SALVATION IS OF THE JEWS

It was to Abraham, from whose loins the Jewish people would come, to whom the knowledge was given as it regards *"Justification by Faith."* In fact, the entirety of the Word of God was given to the Jews. The only writer that may have been Gentile was Luke; however, it is my opinion that Luke, as well, was Jewish. Irrespective, with Israel having the Word of God, it put them light years ahead of any other nation or group of nations in the entirety of the world. Above all of that, they served as the womb of the Messiah, the Lord Jesus Christ. Regrettably, they would not accept Him, which has consigned them now to some 2,000 years of suffering and pain. Still, He did what He came to do, which was to serve as a Sacrifice for the whole of humanity, both Jews and Gentiles.

Jesus told the Samaritan woman, *"You worship you know not what . . ."* (Jn. 4:22), and that's the way it is with every religion in the world, even parts of Christianity, such as Catholicism, Mormonism, etc. They *"worship they know not what."*

Of course, due to the fact of Israel rejecting Christ, they, as well, at this present time, *"worship they know not what."*

ANIMOSITY

So, despite the fact that Bible Christianity has been instrumental in bringing freedom and prosperity to the world, still, there is an embedded animosity in the hearts of most all the unredeemed against those who claim Christ.

Years ago, I was somewhat naïve as it regarded this particular problem. I thought if we were perfectly honest with the news media, showed them exactly what they asked to see, and were totally up front with them, they would in turn be the same with us. To my dismay, I found that was not the case. In other words, their minds were made up before the interview even began. Unfortunately, as Preachers of the Gospel, we have at times furnished the ammunition for the news media to take the direction which they desire. We have only ourselves to blame for that. However, please understand, the more of God that a person has, the more he will be blacklisted, hated, and despised by the news media and much of the world. In fact, at this present time, there are powerful forces in America, who are doing everything within their power to erase God out of anything that pertains to public life and living. Of course, their ambition is to stop all Gospel whatsoever except the brand they choose, whatever that might be. Unfortunately, at the present time, the church is playing right into their hands.

A PERSONAL EXAMPLE

Back in the 1980's, this Ministry (Jimmy Swaggart Ministries), built 144 schools in Third World countries. Actually, some 39 schools were built in Haiti alone.

For the most part, these were schools that only went through the sixth grade. We would run two sessions a day to crowd in as many kids as possible. We would even furnish a hot meal at noon each day, many times, the only meal these kids would get all day long.

Public broadcasting did a program on our schools (or I should say, school), which they aired over one station in the U.S., evidently, with plans to air it nationwide.

At any rate, they claimed that we had only built one school, and that was for rich children.

We contacted the PBS station over which the program aired and furnished the proof of the number of schools we had then built and were building, and that none of them were for rich kids, etc.

To the credit of the station, they made a public apology over the station, and in their response to us, exclaimed their surprise that PBS would falsify a program as they had done.

Why would they want to do this?

It's the animosity of which I speak! Some country western singer could give $50 for something in a Third World country, and it would be played up to the hilt. We could build all of these schools and not only would nothing positive be said, but every effort would be made to discredit what we were doing.

ISRAEL

As we have previously stated, about the only friends that Israel has in the world today are Canada and the USA, and, regrettably, it seems that our support, at least according to this present Administration, is beginning to weaken.

In 2008, there was an economic downturn in the United States because of mortgages on millions of houses, which were bogus. If it is to be noticed, Canada was not touched with that. I wonder if, in the Mind of God, her support of Israel had something to do with that. I also wonder if the animosity toward Israel shown by the Obama Administration has something to do with our own economic downturn. As we have already stated, the Lord meant what He said, and He, in essence, said that He would bless those who blessed Israel and would curse those who cursed Israel (Gen. 12:3).

THE FUTURE OF ISRAEL

Despite the fact of Israel turning her back upon God and crucifying her Messiah, Who just happened to be the Lord of Glory, still, the Lord made many promises to the Patriarchs and the Prophets of old. The truth is, in the coming Kingdom Age, Israel will be the leading Nation in the world. That may be hard to realize when we consider how tiny that modern Israel is. Actually, Israel proper has approximately six million population. There are approximately 14 million more scattered all over the world, with the greatest number being in America, which makes a total of some 20 million. When it is considered that basically two-thirds of those living in Israel will die during the coming Great Tribulation, this only leaves approximately two million in Israel proper. Nevertheless, when Jesus Christ comes back, then every Jew on the face of the Earth will accept Him as Saviour, Lord, and Messiah. As well, they will learn to their chagrin that the One they crucified nearly 2,000 years ago was, in fact, their Messiah and their Lord. Every evidence is that, every Jew on the face of the Earth will, at that time, accept the Lord. This will be immediately after the Second Coming. In turn, they will finally gain the place and position, which had been promised to the Patriarchs and Prophets so long ago, and which they could have had 2,000 years ago had they only accepted Christ then. Concerning this coming time, the great Prophet Jeremiah said:

"At that time they shall call Jerusalem the Throne of the LORD; and all the nations shall be gathered unto it, to the Name of the LORD, to Jerusalem: neither shall they walk anymore after the imagination of their evil heart" (Jer. 3:17). The short phrase, *"At that time,"* refers to the coming Kingdom Age when Christ will reign supreme from Jerusalem and, in reality, over the entirety of the world. In fact, the city of Jerusalem will, at that time, serve as the capital city of the world and, actually, of His Throne.

Concerning that coming day, the great Prophet Ezekiel said:

EZEKIEL

Regarding World War II, days after Germany surrendered, an American general was looking through one of the concentration camps. He stood staring at the most gruesome sight he had ever seen, looking at hundreds and hundreds of Jewish bodies that had been butchered by Adolf Hitler and his henchmen. The world was shortly to find out that some six million Jews had been slaughtered. As the American general stood looking at this gruesome sight that met his eyes, he said the words of Ezekiel came to his mind, *". . . Son of man, can these bones live? And I answered, O Lord GOD, You know"* (Ezek. 37:3).

And then the Lord spoke to the great Prophet and said:

"Therefore prophesy and say unto them, Thus says the Lord GOD; Behold, O My People, I will open your graves, and cause you to come up out of your graves, and bring you into the land of Israel. *(As Prophecy sometimes does, the previous Verse spoke of the last few months or even weeks before the Coming of the Lord and, therefore, the relief of Israel, whereas Verse 12, which we have just quoted, goes back even to World War II and forward.)*

"And you shall know that I am the LORD, when

I have opened your graves, O My People, and brought you up out of your graves *('And brought you up out of your graves,' has reference in totality to the fact that Israel, and for all practical purposes, in the Battle of Armageddon is all but totally destroyed; actually, there is no earthly way they can be salvaged. However, there is a Heavenly Way! And that Heavenly Way is Christ),*

"And shall put My Spirit in you, and you shall live, and I shall place you in your own land: then shall you know that I the LORD have spoken it, and performed it, says the LORD. *(This Passage signals the great Revival that will take place in Israel at the Coming of the Lord. Zechariah gave in greater detail the happening of this great Moving of the Holy Spirit [Zech. 12:10-14; 13:1, 9])"* **(Ezek. 37:12-14).**

HOSEA

Concerning the restoration of Israel, the great Prophet Hosea said this:

"Come, and let us return unto the LORD: for He has torn, and He will heal us; He has smitten, and He will bind us up. *(This speaks of Israel in the last half of the Great Tribulation, under great persecution, finally turning back to the Lord. And how do we know that? We know it because Israel as a Nation has never come to the Lord in the fashion represented here, but which they will do immediately before and after the Second Coming [Zech. 13:1].)*

"After two days will He revive us: in the third day He will raise us up, and we shall live in His Sight. *(Verse 2, which we have just quoted, could very well apply prophetically to the period of Israel's subjection, affliction, and Restoration. Her subjection has lasted 2,000 years, or nearly so [in Biblical Prophecy, two days], and her Millennial Reign will last for 1,000 years [the third day].*

"The word 'day' normally refers to a twenty-four hour

period of time. However, it can be, and often is, used figuratively for a specified or unspecified period of time.

"'In the third day He will raise us up,' refers to the Second Coming of Christ when He will deliver Israel from the Antichrist)" **(Hos. 6:1-2).**

THE PROPHET JOEL

The Holy Spirit through Joel said:

"And I will restore to you the years that the locust has eaten, the cankerworm, and the caterpillar, and the palmerworm, My great Army which I sent among you. *('And I will restore to you the years,' refers to that period of time which began with Nebuchadnezzar and which now has lasted for about 2,500 years. The mention of the 'locust,' etc., is meant to be symbolic of the years lost to the 'times of the Gentiles.' The phrase, 'My great Army which I sent among you,' speaks of the great empires which ruled Israel because of Israel's sin and refusal to repent.)*

"And you shall eat in plenty, and be satisfied, and praise the Name of the LORD your God, Who has dealt wondrously with you: and My People shall never be ashamed. *(Now, Israel will function as she should; as a result, they will 'eat in plenty, and be satisfied.' As well, never again will God's Chosen People 'be ashamed.')*

"And you shall know that I am in the midst of Israel, and that I am the LORD your God, and none else: and My People shall never be ashamed. *(Once again, the Holy Spirit through the Prophet uses the phrase, 'And My People shall never be ashamed,' because Israel, in fact, has lived in 'shame' for over 2,500 years)"* **(Joel 2:25-27).**

THE PROPHET ISAIAH

Isaiah had more to say about the coming Kingdom Age than any other Prophet. Much of his Prophecies concerned

Israel. He said:

"The word that Isaiah the son of Amoz saw concerning Judah and Jerusalem. *(The word 'saw,' as used here by Isaiah, basically means the same thing as 'Vision.')*

"And it shall come to pass in the last days, that the mountain of the LORD's House shall be established in the top of the mountains, and shall be exalted above the hills; and all nations shall flow unto it. *(Verses 2 through 4 in this Chapter correspond to Mic. 4:1-3. Micah's Prophecy was 17 years later than Isaiah's. Some wonder if the latter Prophet borrowed from the former, but this shows a want of intelligence. When God repeats a message, the repetition emphasizes its preciousness to Him and its importance to man.*

"In both of the Prophecies, Isaiah and Micah, the Lord reveals the character of the Kingdom He proposed to set up on the Earth; in the latter, it is repeated to the nations. All of this will take place in the coming Kingdom Age.)

"And many people shall go and say, Come you, and let us go up to the mountain of the LORD, to the House of the God of Jacob; and He will teach us of His Ways, and we will walk in His Paths: for out of Zion shall go forth the Law, and the Word of the LORD from Jerusalem. *(The 'Law,' as referred to here, has no reference to the Law of Moses, but rather to instruction, direction, and teaching. Again, this is the coming Kingdom Age when the Messiah, 'The Greater than Solomon,' will rule the world by Wisdom, Grace and Love.)*

"And He shall judge among the nations, and shall rebuke many people: and they shall beat their swords into plowshares, and their spears into pruninghooks: nation shall not lift up sword against nation, neither shall they learn war any more" (Isa. 2:1-4).

JUDGMENT OF THE NATIONS

In fact, when Jesus Christ comes back to this Earth, which

will be in the midst of the Battle of Armageddon, and which will signal the beginning of the great Kingdom Age, He is going to judge the nations of the world as nations.

Why?

Those nations that at least remained neutral toward Israel during the last half of the Great Tribulation will be treated kindly. The nations that threw in their lot with the Antichrist will actually cease to be as a nation. That's what the Lord thinks of Israel, and every nation in the world at that time, and even of this time, should consider what the Word of God says about the matter. I quote:

> "When the Son of Man shall come in His Glory, and all the Holy Angels with Him, then shall He sit upon the Throne of His Glory *(the Second Coming)*:
>
> "And before Him shall be gathered all nations: and He shall separate them one from another, as a shepherd divides *his* sheep from the goats *(this is called the 'judgment of the nations,' which will commence at the outset, as stated, of the Kingdom Age)*:"

THE SHEEP NATIONS AND THE GOAT NATIONS

> "And He shall set the sheep on His Right Hand *(refers to nations which would not cooperate with the Antichrist)*, but the goats on the left *(nations which cooperated with the Antichrist)*.
>
> "Then shall the King *(the Lord Jesus Christ)* say unto them on His Right Hand, Come, you blessed of My Father, inherit the Kingdom prepared for you from the foundation of the world *(this has nothing to do with Salvation, but rather these particular nations being allowed to enter into the Kingdom Age)*:
>
> "For I was hungry, and you gave Me meat: I was thirsty, and you gave Me drink: I was a stranger, and you took Me in *(although the adage proves true for all time, Christ is basically here speaking of Israel and her treatment by various nations during the Great Tribulation)*:

"Naked, and you clothed Me: I was sick, and you visited Me: I was in prison, and you came unto Me.

"Then shall the righteous answer Him, saying, Lord, when did we see You hungry, and fed *You*? or thirsty, and gave *You* drink? *(The word, 'righteous,' does not pertain to the Righteousness of Christ given to Believers at Salvation, but instead, righteous dealings with Israel by these nations.)*"

YOU!

"When saw we You a stranger, and took You in? or naked, and clothed *You*?

"Or when did we see You sick, or in prison, and came unto You?

"And the King shall answer and say unto them, Verily I say unto you, Inasmuch as you have done *it* unto one of the least of these My Brethren, you have done *it* unto Me *(as stated, the adage holds true for all time, but Christ is primarily speaking here of Israel and the help given her by certain nations during the Great Tribulation).*"

EVERLASTING FIRE

"Then shall He say also unto them on the left hand *(the goat nations)*, Depart from Me, you cursed, into everlasting fire, prepared for the devil and his angels *(nations that hindered or tried to harm Israel during the Great Tribulation)*:

"For I was hungry, and you gave Me no meat: I was thirsty, and you gave Me no drink:

"I was a stranger, and you took Me not in: naked, and you clothed Me not: sick, and in prison, and you visited Me not.

"Then shall they also answer Him, saying, Lord, when did we see You hungry, or thirsty, or a stranger, or naked, or sick, or in prison, and did not minister unto You?

"Then shall He answer them, saying, Verily I say unto you, Inasmuch as you did *it* not to one of the least of these, you did *it* not to Me *(to bless one who belongs to God is to bless God; to harm one who belongs to God is to harm God; we see here the results of such action)*."

LIFE ETERNAL

"And these shall go away into everlasting punishment: but the righteous into life eternal *(all of this will happen soon after the Second Coming; the leaders of the nations, who tried to help the Antichrist against Israel during the Great Tribulation, will evidently be executed and, consequently, will die eternally lost; conversely, the leaders of the nations, who tried to help Israel at that time, will be given an opportunity to accept Christ as Saviour, which they, no doubt, will and will, thereby, be given 'life eternal')*" (Mat. 25:31-46).

All of this means that Israel, as tiny as she might be, is not just another nation in the world. These people were chosen by God for a special purpose, and, to be sure, they have contributed greatly to the positive welfare of the entirety of civilization. In fact, no group of people can match their contributions, and I might quickly add, positive contributions, to society as a whole.

A PERSONAL EXPERIENCE

Some years ago, 1987, if I remember correctly, I was asked to address a small Jewish gathering in Baton Rouge, Louisiana, with the main speaker being the future Prime Minister of Israel. He made a statement I've never forgotten.

He named several very famous Jewish scientists, doctors, etc., and noted what they had contributed to society. He mentioned

Jonas Salk, who developed the serum stopping the polio germ, and then asked the question, *"How many Jews, who could have made a contribution to society, such as Jonas Salk, were, instead, slaughtered in the concentration camps of Adolf Hitler?"*

I was listening to a particular radio program some time back when the host made mention of the fact that the Jews had received some 30 Noble Prizes, if I remember the number correctly, in a certain span of time. He noted that the world of Islam had only received two, I believe he said. At any rate, the disparity between the numbers spoke volumes.

Yes, there is a hatred for Israel in the world today, which will come to a head under the Antichrist. However, that hatred will change when Jesus Christ comes back, and come back He shall!

CHAPTER FOUR

THE REASON FOR ARMAGEDDON

Some 2,500 years ago, the Holy Spirit gave us insight as to the thinking of the coming man of sin as it regards Israel. While in the Prophecies of Ezekiel, He doesn't tell us the real reason, He, however, does give us some preliminary knowledge. We will look at the reason a little later.

THE WORD OF THE LORD

We are quoting the Text and the notes directly from THE EXPOSITOR'S STUDY BIBLE. It says:

"And the Word of the LORD came unto me, saying,

"Son of man, set your face against Gog, the land of Magog, the chief prince of Meshech and Tubal, and prophesy against him *('Gog' is another name for the Antichrist)*,

"And say, Thus says the Lord GOD; Behold, I am against you, O Gog, the chief prince of Meshech and Tubal *(for many years, Bible teachers have thought that these Passages referred to Russia, but a closer investigation of the statements prove otherwise; therefore, the phrase, 'Behold, I am against you, O Gog,' is not referring to Russia, but instead, to the Antichrist)*:

"And I will turn you back, and put hooks into your jaws, and I will bring you forth, and all your army, horses and horsemen, all of them clothed with all sorts of armour, even a great company with bucklers and shields, all of them handling swords *(this Prophecy refers to the Battle of Armageddon, which will be the second invasion by the Antichrist of Israel, in which he will be totally destroyed. The first invasion will take place in the midst of the Great Tribulation when the Antichrist will then show his true colors)*:

"Persia, Ethiopia, and Libya with them; all of them with shield and helmet:

"Gomer, and all his bands; the house of Togarmah of the north quarters, and all his bands: and many people with you. *(These Passages merely reinforce the statements previously made, that the army of the Antichrist will consist of people from many countries, including Russia.)*

"Be you prepared, and prepare for yourself, you, and all your company who are assembled unto you, and be you a guard unto them. *('Be you prepared,' merely refers to a taunt given by the Holy Spirit to the Antichrist. In other words, 'Prepare yourself to the very best of your ability, and still it will avail you nothing as you will be totally defeated')*" **(Ezek. 38:1-7).**

GOG TO INVADE ISRAEL IN THE LAST DAYS

To which we briefly alluded in the notes regarding Verse 3, for years preachers tried to force these Passages into Russia. I even read articles where the names, *"Meshech"* and *"Tubal,"* were changed by these so-called Prophecy teachers to *"Moscow"* and *"Tobolsk."*

In fact, there were many preachers who claimed that Ezekiel,

Chapters 38 and 39, had to do with an attack by Russia against Israel, claiming that it had nothing to do with the Battle of Armageddon.

I suppose those preachers never bothered to look at the chronology of these Chapters. When this Battle is over, which, incidentally, it most definitely will be the Battle of Armageddon, we find the Prophet immediately taking us into the Millennium. He then gives a vivid description of the City of Jerusalem as it will be in the coming Kingdom Age, and the rebuilt Temple. This spans Ezekiel, Chapters 40 through 48, and immediately follows Chapters 38 and 39, which portray the Battle of Armageddon. As stated, all they had to do was to look at the chronology of these Chapters, and it would have quickly become evident that the great Prophet is speaking of the Battle of Armageddon in Chapters 38 and 39.

In 1989, the Soviet Union collapsed, with a form of democracy then coming to Russia and its satellites. So much for these former prognostications.

THE LATTER YEARS

"After many days you shall be visited: in the latter years you shall come into the land that is brought back from the sword, and is gathered out of many people, against the mountains of Israel, which have been always waste: but it is brought forth out of the nations, and they shall dwell safely all of them. *(The two phrases, 'After many days' and 'In the latter years,' refer to this present time and the immediate future; therefore, any claims that this Chapter has already been fulfilled are spurious.*

" 'The land that is brought back from the sword,' refers to the many conflicts Israel has had since becoming a Nation in 1948.

" 'And is gathered out of many people,' refers to the various nations, such as Egypt, Syria, Iraq, etc., which did not desire Israel to become a Nation, and which, therefore,

greatly opposed her.

" 'But it is brought forth out of the nations,' pertains to the United Nations voting that Israel would become a State, with even Russia voting her approval.

" 'And they shall dwell safely all of them,' refers to the terrible horror of the Holocaust in World War II, with some six million Jews being slaughtered by Hitler, and Israel then demanding a homeland instead of being scattered all over the world. Their feeling was that if this could be obtained, then they would be 'safe.')"

THE INVASION

"You shall ascend and come like a storm, you shall be like a cloud to cover the land, you, and all your bands, and many people with you. *(As stated, this is the Battle of Armageddon.)*

"Thus says the Lord GOD; It shall also come to pass, that at the same time shall things come into your mind, and you shall think an evil thought *(the 'evil thought' will consist of the plans of the Antichrist, inspired of Satan, to destroy Israel and the Jews. That plan, as stated, is the Battle of Armageddon!):"*

AND YOU SHALL SAY . . .

"And you shall say, I will go up to the land of unwalled villages; I will go to them who are at rest, who dwell safely, all of them dwelling without walls, and having neither bars nor gates *(the phrases, 'The land of unwalled villages,' 'Dwelling without walls,' and 'Having neither bars nor gates,' refer to Israel's efforts at mobilization to be rather weak, at least in the mind of the Antichrist)*,

"To take a spoil, and to take a prey; to turn your hand upon the desolate places that are now inhabited, and upon the people who are gathered out of the nations, which

have gotten cattle and goods, who dwell in the midst of the land. *(This is the invasion of Israel by the Antichrist, called the 'Battle of Armageddon,' which will precipitate the Second Coming of the Lord.)*

"Sheba, and Dedan, and the merchants of Tarshish, with all the young lions thereof, shall say unto you, Are you come to take a spoil? have you gathered your company to take a prey? to carry away silver and gold, to take away cattle and goods, to take a great spoil? *(The questions asked by these particular nations are not meant to proclaim an adversarial position; in fact, they will probably throw in their lot with the Antichrist, hoping to get a part of the 'great spoil')*" **(Ezek. 38:8-13).**

GOG'S ATTACK AGAINST GOD'S LAND

"Therefore, son of man, prophesy and say unto Gog, Thus says the Lord GOD; In that day when My People of Israel dwell safely, shall you not know it? *(The idea of this Verse is: despite the Antichrist invading Israel and defeating her at the midpoint of the Great Tribulation, thereby breaking his seven-year pact, still, due to him having pressing business elsewhere [Dan. 11:44], Israel will then filter back into the land, reoccupying it, and seemingly will dwell safely. This will, no doubt, infuriate the 'man of sin,' and he will set about to handle the situation once and for all!)*"

A GREAT COMPANY, AND A MIGHTY ARMY

"And you shall come from your place out of the north parts, you, and many people with you, all of them riding upon horses, a great company, and a mighty army *(the 'north parts' do not refer to Russia, as some think, but rather to Syria. In fact, the Antichrist [Gog] will come from Syria; however, the Syria of Daniel's Prophecies, of* *which this speaks, included modern Syria, Iraq, and Iran)*:

"And you shall come up against My People of Israel, as a cloud to cover the land; it shall be in the latter days, and I will bring you against My Land, that the heathen may know Me, when I shall be sanctified in you, O Gog, before their eyes. *('In the latter days,' refers to the last of the last days, which pertain to the present and near future. In other words, these Prophecies have already begun to come to pass, and, with each passing day, will accelerate their fulfillment)*" (Ezek. 38:14-16).

MANY PROPHECIES TO BE FULFILLED

"Thus says the Lord GOD; Are you he of whom I have spoken in old time by My Servants the Prophets of Israel, which prophesied in those days many years that I would bring you against them? *(The Lord is actually speaking here of the Prophecies given to Ezekiel, of which this is one, as well as those of Isaiah, Daniel, Zechariah, and others!)*" (Ezek. 38:17).

WHAT IS THE MAIN REASON FOR ARMAGEDDON?

It is the ambition of the Antichrist to rule the world, which he will come close to doing but for the Second Coming of our Lord. It must be quickly added that the hatred he has in his heart for Israel is placed there by his unholy sponsor, Satan. As we've already said in this Volume, Satan wants to be God. He said, and as recorded by Isaiah:

"For you have said in your heart, I will ascend into Heaven, I will exalt my throne above the stars of God: I will sit also upon the mount of the congregation, in the sides of the north:

"I will ascend above the heights of the clouds; I will be like the Most High" (Isa. 14:13-14).

How does he think that he can do this?

He knows that he is but a creature and that God is the Creator.

As such, God is Omnipotent, meaning all-powerful, Omniscient, meaning all-knowing, and Omnipresent, meaning everywhere. So, how in the world does he hope to gain ascendancy over God and actually become God himself?

He knows that all the Lord has to do is simply speak the word, and he is gone. So, understanding this, and he understands it better than any human being, how does he think that he can accomplish what he has set out to do?

To be sure, the Evil One most definitely does believe that he can accomplish this task. Despite Who God is and despite Calvary, which, in essence, totally defeated Satan (Col. 2:14-15), despite all of that and so much more of which we have no knowledge, he still thinks he can come out ahead. In fact, his greatest effort, which will be the Antichrist, is just ahead.

Of course, many ask the question, *"Cannot Satan read the Bible?"* Most definitely, he can read, and he is very, very intelligent. But, the truth is, he, like all of his followers, simply don't believe the Bible. He knows exactly what the Bible says about him and his followers. He is very well acquainted with the following Passages:

> **"And I saw an Angel come down from Heaven** *(continues with the idea that Angels are very prominent in the Plan and Work of God)*, **having the key of the bottomless pit** *(speaks of the same place recorded in Rev. 9:1; however, there the key is given to Satan, but this Angel of Rev. 20:1 'has the key,' implying that he has had it all along; more than likely, God allows this Angel to give the key to Satan in Rev. 9:1)* **and a great chain in his hand** *(should be taken literally)*.
>
> **"And he laid hold on the dragon, that old serpent, which is the Devil, and Satan** *(as a 'dragon,' he shows his power; as a 'serpent,' he shows his cunning; as the 'Devil,' he is the accuser; and as 'Satan,' he is the adversary)*, **and bound him a thousand years** *(refers to being bound by the great chain carried by the Angel)*,

"And cast him into the bottomless pit, and shut him up, and set a seal upon him *(speaks of the abyss being sealed to keep him there)*, that he should deceive the nations no more, till the thousand years should be fulfilled: and after that he must be loosed a little season. *(At the end of the thousand-year period, Satan will be loosed out of his prison. He will make another attempt to deceive the nations, in which he will not succeed. We aren't told how long this 'little season' will be)*" **(Rev. 20:1-3).**

THE LAKE OF FIRE

The Evil One also knows what the Bible says about him regarding his eternal destiny, but, as stated, he simply doesn't believe it. John wrote:

"And the Devil who deceived them was cast into the Lake of Fire and brimstone *(marks the end of Satan regarding his influence in the world, and, in fact, in any part of the Creation of God)*, where the Beast and the False Prophet are *(proclaims the fact that these two were placed in 'the Lake of Fire and Brimstone' some 1,000 years earlier [Rev. 19:20])*, and shall be tormented day and night forever and ever. *(This signifies the eternity of this place. It is a matter of interest to note that Satan's first act is recorded in Genesis, Chapter 3 [the third Chapter from the beginning], whereas his last act on a worldwide scale is mentioned in Revelation, Chapter 20 [the third Chapter from the end])*" **(Rev. 20:10).**

To understand a little more about our adversary, perhaps it would be of benefit to portray that which Ezekiel gave us as it regards this unholy creature, who has caused so much pain and suffering in this world. The great Prophet said:

SATAN

"Moreover, the Word of the LORD came unto me,

saying *(the tenor of this Chapter will now change from the earthly monarch, the 'prince of Tyre,' to his sponsor, Satan, of which the earthly king was a symbol),*

"Son of man, take up a lamentation upon the king of Tyrus, and say unto him, Thus says the Lord GOD; You seal up the sum, full of wisdom, and perfect in beauty. *(As is obvious, even though the king of Tyrus is used as a symbol, the statements made could not refer to any mere mortal. In fact, they refer to Satan.*

"The phrase, 'You seal up the sum,' means that Lucifer, when originally created by God, was the perfection of wisdom and beauty. In fact, the phrase intimates that Lucifer was the wisest and most beautiful Angel created by God, and served the Lord in Holiness and Righteousness for a given period of time.

" 'Perfect in beauty,' means that he was the most beautiful of God's Angelic Creation. The Holy Spirit even labeled his beauty as 'perfect.')"

THE CREATION OF SATAN

"You have been in Eden the Garden of God; every precious stone was your covering, the sardius, topaz, and the diamond, the beryl, the onyx, and the jasper, the sapphire, the emerald, and the carbuncle, and gold: the workmanship of your tabrets and of your pipes was prepared in you in the day that you were created. *('You have been in Eden the Garden of God,' does not actually refer to the 'Eden' of Gen., Chpt. 3, but rather to the 'Eden' which existed on this Planet before Adam and Eve, which, evidently, was ruled by Lucifer before his rebellion.*

" 'Every precious stone was your covering,' presents itself as very similar to the dress of the High Priest of Israel [Ex. 28:17-20].

" 'The workmanship of your tabrets and of your pipes,' has to do with music. There is every indication that Lucifer's

leadership had something to do with the Worship of God. As well, he is called, 'O Lucifer, son of the morning' [Isa. 14:12]. When the Earth was originally created, the Scripture says, 'The morning stars sang together, and all the sons of God shouted for joy' [Job 38:4-7]. So, if the idiom, 'son of the morning,' can be linked to the 'morning stars,' these Passages tell us that Lucifer, at least before his fall, was greatly used in leading the Worship of God.

"In fact, this is the reason that Satan has done everything within his power to corrupt the music of the world and to corrupt the music of the Church above all. Inasmuch as the Book of Psalms is the longest Book in the Bible, we learn from this that music and singing are among the highest forms of Worship, if not the highest form of Worship, of the Lord.)"

THE ANOINTED CHERUB

"You are the anointed Cherub who covers; and I have set you so: you were upon the Holy Mountain of God; you have walked up and down in the midst of the stones of fire. *('You are the anointed Cherub who covers,' means that Lucifer was chosen and 'anointed' by God for a particular task and service. This probably was the 'worship' to which we have just alluded.*

" 'You were upon the Holy Mountain of God,' speaks of his place and position relative to the Throne [Rev. 4:2-11]. 'You have walked up and down in the midst of the stones of fire,' has reference to his nearness to the Throne [Ezek. 1:26-27]. As well, the phrase, 'Walked up and down,' seems to imply that not just any Angel would have been given such latitude.)"

INIQUITY

"You were perfect in your ways from the day that

you were created, till iniquity was found in you. *(Pride was the form of this iniquity [Lk. 10:17-18]; the rebellion of Lucifer against God probably caused the catastrophe, which occurred between the First and Second Verses of Gen., Chpt. 1.)*

"By the multitude of your merchandise they have filled the midst of you with violence, and you have sinned; therefore I will cast you as profane out of the Mountain of God: and I will destroy you, O covering Cherub, from the midst of the stones of fire. *('Violence' has been the earmark of Satan's rule and reign in the world of darkness [Jn. 10:10]. Lucifer being 'cast out' of the 'Mountain of God' refers to him losing his place and position, which he had held with God since his creation. It was because 'he had sinned,' which spoke of pride that caused him to lift himself up against God.)"*

PRIDE

"Your heart was lifted up because of your beauty, you have corrupted your wisdom by reason of your brightness: I will cast you to the ground, I will lay you before kings, that they may behold you. *('Your heart was lifted up because of your beauty,' tells us the reason for his fall. As stated, it was pride. He took his eyes off of Christ, noticing his own beauty as it grew more and more glorious in his eyes. At some point in time, his 'heart' was changed from Christ to himself. As far as we know, this was the origin of evil in all of God's Creation.*

" 'You have corrupted your wisdom by reason of your brightness,' does not refer to the loss of wisdom but, instead, refers to wisdom corrupted, hence, the insidious design practiced upon the human family [Jn. 10:10].

" 'I will cast you to the ground,' refers to his ultimate defeat [Rev. 12:7-12]. 'I will lay you before kings, that they may behold you,' refers to him ultimately being cast

into the Lake of Fire, where all the kings of the Earth who have died lost will behold him in his humiliation [Mat. 25:41; Rev. 20:10].)"

NEVER SHALL YOU BE ANYMORE

"**You have defiled your sanctuaries by the multitude of your iniquities, by the iniquity of your traffic; therefore will I bring forth a fire from the midst of you, it shall devour you, and I will bring you to ashes upon the Earth in the sight of all them who behold you.** *(When Satan at long last will be thrown into the Lake of Fire [Rev. 20:10], all the billions he has duped, who also are in Hell because of him, will hate him with a passion that words cannot begin to express, and a hatred which will last forever and forever.)*

"**All they who know you among the people shall be astonished at you: you shall be a terror, and never shall you be any more.** *(Then the prayer of Christ, 'Your Will be done in Earth, as it is in Heaven,' will finally be answered and brought to pass [Mat. 6:9-10])*" **(Ezek. 28:11-19).**

SO, WHAT IS THE REAL REASON FOR ARMAGEDDON?

As is obvious, to annihilate every Jew and to take the land of Israel in totality will be the grand design and purpose of the Evil One.

The reason for that is that the Word of God may fall to the ground, so to speak.

There are more predictions in the Bible concerning the Restoration of Israel, of which we have named just a few, than any other Prophecy. If Satan can destroy the Jews and take the land of Israel, this will circumvent the Word of God and prove it to be a lie. If that happens, Satan has gained his unholy end; he is now God of the Universe.

David said:

"I will worship toward Your Holy Temple, and praise Your Name for Your Lovingkindness and for Your Truth: for You have magnified Your Word above all Your Name. *(His Name means His Reputation and Character for faithfulness and goodness. His Word is His Promise. In that future day, His Performance will exceed His Promise, thereby, magnifying His Word above all His Name)*" (Ps. 138:2).

So, that is the motive behind Satan's madness. Knowing that the Restoration of Israel is addressed in the Bible more so than any other Promise or Prophecy, the Evil One reasons in his mind that if he can cause that Prophecy to fail, he will have won the day.

ADOLF HITLER

World War II was far more spiritual than most realize. Satan knew that the United States was going to play the greatest part ever in world Evangelism, which would come up during the 1960's through the 1980's. So, he set it in the minds of the Japanese to destroy America.

As it regards Germany, Satan put it in the heart of Adolf Hitler and his henchmen to annihilate the Jews. The Evil One knew that the time of their Restoration, referring to its beginning, was to take place shortly. If enough Jews could be slaughtered, this would mean there would not be enough for a Nation to be formed.

Toward the close of the war, when fuel and raw materials were in extremely short supply for Germany, they still kept the trains rolling. They were filled with hundreds of thousands of Jewish refugees being taken to the concentration camps where they would be gassed to death. In other words, he deprived his armies of much needed material in order that Jews be slaughtered. He did not succeed, but it was not for a lack of trying. Of course, as everyone knows, the Jews formed a Nation in 1948, and did so in the face of overwhelming odds.

THE ANTICHRIST

In his effort to take over the entirety of the world, many may wonder as to why the Antichrist will devote the power of his army to the destruction of Israel, considering that he has just overpowered Russia and possibly China as well. Of course, Satan will be inspiring and directing him, and that includes the most powerful fallen Angels under Satan's domain.

THE SPIRIT WORLD OF DARKNESS

John the Beloved gives us more information concerning the Antichrist, and above all, the Spirit world of darkness that will propel him to his place and position. In other words, as previously stated, the Antichrist will have the entirety of the power of Satan behind him and, as well, all of the powerful fallen Angels, which will give him wisdom and ability.

The entirety of the Book of Revelation is written from the perspective of the spirit world. As such, it is very difficult to understand. That which I'm about to give, which will come from the Thirteenth Chapter of Revelation, would little be understandable for most were it not for the notes in THE EXPOSITOR'S STUDY BIBLE. However, to show the power of this man of sin, who is soon to come upon this Earth, I think the information that John the Beloved gave us will be beneficial. He said:

"**And I stood upon the sand of the sea** *(not a body of water but a sea of people)*, **and saw a beast rise up out of the sea** *(pertains to the Antichrist, now empowered by Satan as no other man ever has been)*, **having seven heads and ten horns** *(represents seven empires that have greatly persecuted Israel in the past, with the 'ten horns' actually being the seventh head; the 'ten horns' representing ten nations are yet future)*, **and upon his horns ten crowns** *(the horns now being crowned show that these ten nations have now come to power and will use that power to help the Antichrist; they will be located in the Middle East and in parts of Europe and possibly North Africa, all being in the old Roman Empire territory [Dan. 7:7-8])*, **and upon his heads the name of blasphemy.** *(Satan controlled these empires and will control the ten nations, therefore, the name 'blasphemy.')*"

THE POWERFUL FALLEN ANGEL

"And the beast which I saw *(represents the fallen Angel who will be let out of the bottomless pit to help the Antichrist [Rev. 11:7]; both the fallen Angel and the Antichrist are referred to as a 'beast,' but they are two different beings)* **was like unto a leopard** *(this fallen Angel will help the Antichrist to speedily conquer; Daniel describes this event as well [Dan. 7:6])*, **and his feet were as *the feet* of a bear** *(carries the characteristics of the ancient Medo-Persian Empire, which is ferociousness)*, **and his mouth as the mouth of a lion** *(portrays the finesse, grandeur, and pomp of the Babylonian Empire)*: **and the dragon** *(Satan)* **gave him** *(the Antichrist)* **his power, and his seat, and great authority.** *(So, the Antichrist will have Satan helping him as well as this powerful fallen Angel and, no doubt, a host of other fallen Angels and demon spirits.)*"

THE FALLEN ANGEL WHO HELPED ALEXANDER THE GREAT

"And I saw one of his heads as it were wounded to death *(doesn't refer to the Antichrist, but rather one of the empires of the past, which greatly persecuted Israel; it pertains to the Grecian Empire under Alexander the Great and, in reality, speaks of the same fallen Angel helping Alexander; when Alexander died, this fallen Angel, who* *helped him to conquer so speedily, was locked away in the bottomless pit, which is that to which the first phrase of this Third Verse is addressing [Dan. 7:6])*; **and his deadly wound was healed** *(refers to the fact that this fallen Angel will be released out of the bottomless pit to aid and abet the Antichrist [Rev., Chpt. 17]; it is doubtful the Antichrist will know or realize the source of his power, taking all the credit unto himself)*: **and all the world wondered after the beast.** *(This refers to the part of the world he has conquered, but with the entirety of the world definitely paying him homage as he now seems to exude superhuman ability.)*"

WORSHIP OF THE BEAST

"**And they worshipped the dragon which gave power unto the beast** *(refers to the fact that men worship power, in this case, worshipping Satan)*: **and they worshipped the beast, saying, Who *is* like unto the beast? who is able to make war with him?** *(This proclaims the means by which power is worshipped.)*

"**And there was given unto him a mouth speaking great things and blasphemies** *(powerful claims will be made, with the Name of Jesus being ridiculed)*; **and power was given unto him to continue forty *and* two months** *(the last three and one half years of the Great Tribulation; despite the power of the Antichrist, the Lord still controls the time frames and, in fact, all events)*.

"**And he opened his mouth in blasphemy against God, to blaspheme His Name** *(he will use all the power of print, radio, television, and computers to demean the God of the Bible; it will be a regimen of blasphemy on a worldwide basis such as the world has never known before)*, **and His Tabernacle** *(refers to Heaven)*, **and them who dwell in Heaven.** *(Even though it refers to all Believers in Heaven, pointedly, it refers to the 144,000 Jews who have been raptured and are now in Heaven. The insults will be* *thick and fast, in effect, ridiculing Heaven.)*"

THE SAINTS

"**And it was given unto him to make war with the Saints, and to overcome them** *(this will include all Believers all over the world; as well, the Text implies by the word 'overcome' that the Lord will allow such to happen)*: **and power was given him over all kindreds, and tongues, and nations.** *(This doesn't include the entirety of the world, but rather the area over which he has control, which is basically the area of the old Roman Empire.)*

"**And all who dwell upon the Earth shall worship him** *(first of all, we're speaking here of worship, not dominion of nations; as well, the word 'all' doesn't refer to every single human being, but rather people from all nations of the world, however many that number might be)*, **whose names are not written in the Book of Life** *(refers to the fact that Believers will not worship the Antichrist)* **of the Lamb slain from the foundation of the world.** *(This tells us that the only way one's name can be placed in the Book of Life is by acceptance of Jesus Christ as one's Lord and Saviour, and what He did for us at the Cross. Also, the phrase, 'From the foundation of the world,' proclaims the fact that the Doctrine of 'Jesus Christ and Him Crucified' is the Foundation Doctrine of all Doctrines. In other words, every Doctrine from the Bible is built on the Foundation of the Cross of Christ, otherwise, it is bogus)*" **(Rev. 13:1-8).**

PRESENT HATRED FOR CHRISTIANITY

Despite the fact of nearly 4,000 Americans slaughtered by Muslims on September 11, 2001 (9/11), believe it or not, there is probably more animosity against Christianity in the United States, that's supposed to be Christian, at least, somewhat,

than against the religion of Islam.

When this demon possessed individual in Norway slaughtered over 90 people, the New York Times labeled him as a *"Christian."* He was not a Christian and had made no profession of being a Christian. So, why did the New York Times desire to paint him as such?

They did so because they hate Christianity, which means they hate the Bible, which means they hate the Lord Jesus Christ. Would to God that it was limited only to this left-wing newspaper, but unfortunately, and, as stated, such animosity against Christianity is shared by many, with it growing more evil and wicked almost by the day.

There has never been anything so obviously hostile to the United States, in a sense, threatening our destruction, as the world of Islam. And yet, our politicians, our leaders, even the preachers, for the most part, don't seem to see the danger. The nation has embraced a Muslim policy that claims while there are a few fanatical Muslims, all the balance constitutes wonderful people. The truth is, there are fanatical Muslims; however, all Muslims subscribe to the Koran, and the Koran demands death to the infidel. An infidel is anyone who isn't a Muslim. The truth is, virtually all Muslims, although not murderers, are, in fact, in sympathy with the murderers. We have conveniently overlooked this glaring truth. Please understand, calling a rattlesnake a poodle dog doesn't change the nature of the rattlesnake.

There are Muslims at this very moment, in obedience to the Koran, who are trying to get their hands on a small atomic bomb. If they can do that, they will gladly incinerate a city in the United States, causing the death of untold thousands. I once thought if that happened, as gruesome as it might be, it might wake America up; however, of late, I have changed my mind. I think, God forbid, that if such a thing happened, the policy of this nation would little change, if at all. The powers that be would claim that it's just the fanatical Muslims doing such a thing, with most Muslims being peace loving people.

It must be understood that Muslims the world over, from the time they are children and able to comprehend anything, are taught to hate Israel and to hate America. In fact, Israel is called *"little Satan,"* while America is called *"great Satan."*

In the public schools of this nation, while the Bible is not allowed to be read, the Koran can be read as much as one desires. In fact, the culture of Islam is actually being taught in some of our schools, and, to be sure, Christianity is not allowed any freedom at all. Little by little, and maybe faster than we realize, America is digging her own grave.

And yet, I do not lay the blame for all of this at the doorstep of the politicians, etc. I lay the blame at the doorstep of the church. As the spirituality of the church, or the lack thereof, so is the spirituality of the nation.

In California, Governor Brown signed into Law that the culture of homosexuality and lesbianism must be taught in the public school system. It won't be long before the entirety of the nation follows suit. As I dictate these notes in July, 2011, some six states now have legalized homosexual marriages. Sooner or later, again, the balance of the states will follow suit. This is a slap in the Face of God.

As a Christian, we aren't opposed to homosexuals because they are human beings like anyone else; however, we are most definitely opposed to homosexuality. The same would go for alcoholics. We aren't opposed to these people, but we are opposed to alcoholism, etc. While Jesus loved the sinner, He hated the sin (Jn. 3:16).

The point of all of this is, society the world over is getting ready for the advent of the Antichrist, whether they know it or not.

MUSLIMS AND THE ANTICHRIST

While the Antichrist will *"use"* the Muslims at first, which we've already addressed, the truth is, ultimately, he will turn on them nearly as much as he will those who are Christians. In fact, he will put down every religion in the world, at least, where he has control, demanding worship himself. The Scripture says of him, *"Who opposes and exalts himself above all that is called God, or that is worshipped; so that he as God sits in the Temple of God, showing himself that he is God"* (II Thess. 2:4). So, he will tolerate no competing religion.

It sobers one to realize that we are closer to these things than ever before.

CHAPTER FIVE

THE LOCATION OF ARMAGEDDON

"And He (God) gathered them together into a place called in the Hebrew tongue Armageddon" (Rev. 16:16).

As we have stated, due to being able to broker a peace treaty between Israel and the Muslim world, the Antichrist will be accepted by Israel as their Messiah. In fact, the first three and a half years of the Great Tribulation period will not be so bad at all for Israel. Actually, the Apostle Paul addressed this when he said:

"For when they shall say, Peace and safety *(refers to Israel but will, as well, characterize the world; it pertains to the Antichrist signing the seven-year pact with Israel and other nations [Dan. 9:27])*; **then sudden destruction comes upon them** *(at the midpoint of the seven-year period, the Antichrist will break his pact, actually invading Israel [Rev. 12:1-6])*, **as travail upon a woman with child; and they shall not escape.** *(The Great Tribulation is definitely coming upon this world [Mat. 24:21])*" **(I Thess. 5:3).**

Actually, I think it would be good for us to give the Biblical account of the Antichrist breaking his agreement with Israel, which he will do at the midpoint. While the account is given in the Book of Revelation, it is given from the perspective of the spirit world. In other words, it shows a behind the scenes look at what actually happens in the spirit world, which precipitates things on Earth. Perhaps the notes that will accompany the Text will help you to understand a little better that which the Holy Spirit is saying as it regards Israel and how her *"messiah"* turned on her.

THE SUN-CLAD WOMAN

"And there appeared a great wonder in Heaven *(should have been translated, 'a great sign in Heaven')*; a woman clothed with the Sun *(speaks of National Israel with the 'Sun' being a symbol of her Glory)*, and the moon under her feet *(speaks of dominion, hence, the mention of her feet)*, and upon her head a crown of twelve stars *(speaks of dominion regained and Israel restored)*:

"And she being with child cried *(pertains to the 144,000 Jews who will be Saved in the first half of the Great Tribulation [Rev., Chpt. 7])*, travailing in birth, and pained to be delivered. *(This concerns spiritual pregnancy, with the agonies of childbirth typifying in the physical what will take place in the spiritual. In other words, the most difficult time for Israel is now about to come upon her, which will be the last half of the Great Tribulation [Isa. 66:7-8].)*"

THE GREAT RED DRAGON

"And there appeared another wonder in Heaven *(should have been translated, 'another sign')*; and behold a great red dragon *(denotes Satan and his murderous purpose, typified by the color of 'red')*, having seven heads *(refers to empires that persecuted Israel, even until John's day; those empires were Egypt, Assyria, Babylon, Medo-Persia, Greece, and Rome)* **and ten horns** *(represents ten nations that will be ruled by the Antichrist in the last days and will greatly persecute Israel; actually, the seventh head is those 'ten horns'; Daniel tells us that these 'ten horns' representing ten nations will be in the old Roman Empire territory, which refers to the Middle East and parts of Europe [Dan. 7:7])*, **and seven crowns upon his heads** *(represents the fact that Satan controlled these particular kingdoms).*"

THE MAN CHILD

"And his tail drew the third part of the stars of Heaven *(this goes all the way back to the original rebellion of Lucifer against God; at that time, one-third of the Angels threw in their lot with him; we know these 'stars' represent Angels because Verse 9 of this Chapter tells us so)*, **and did cast them to the Earth** *(is given to us more clearly in Rev. 12:7-9)*: **and the dragon stood before the woman who was ready to be delivered** *(does not pertain to the birth of Christ as some claim, but rather the man child, which is the 144,000 Jews who will give their hearts to Christ [Rev., Chpt. 7])*, **for to devour her child as soon as it was born.** *(This pertains to the fact that the Antichrist will hate these Jews who have come to Christ. This will take place in the first half of the Great Tribulation and may well be the primary reason the Antichrist will turn on Israel at that time.)*"

CALLED TO RULE

"And she *(Israel)* **brought forth a man child** *(as stated, this is the 144,000 Jews who will come to Christ during the first half of the Great Tribulation [Rev., Chpt. 7]; we aren't told exactly how this will be done)*, **who was to rule all**

nations with a rod of iron *(Israel, under Christ, will definitely fill this role in the coming Millennial Reign):* **and her child was caught up unto God, and *to* His Throne.** *(This refers to the Rapture of the 144,000, which will take place at about the midpoint of the Great Tribulation.)*

"**And the woman fled into the wilderness** *(the 'woman' is National Israel; at the midpoint of the Great Tribulation, the Antichrist will turn on Israel and defeat her, with many thousands of Jews fleeing into the wilderness),* **where she has a place prepared of God** *(this place is actually ancient Petra, located in Jordan [Isa. 16:1-5]),* **that they should feed her there a thousand two hundred *and* threescore days.** *('They' mentioned here refers, oddly enough, to the Arabs of Jordan. The 1,260 days constitute almost all of the last half of the Great Tribulation. Incidentally, Petra is now empty of people, awaiting the arrival of Israel)*" **(Rev. 12:1-6).**

PERSECUTION

"**And when the dragon saw that he was cast unto the Earth, he persecuted the woman who brought forth the man *child*.** *(That's when, as stated, the Antichrist will break his seven-year Covenant with Israel, attacking and defeating her [Dan. 9:27].)*

"**And to the woman were given two wings of a great eagle, that she might fly into the wilderness, into her place** *(the Lord will help Israel at that time, and do so greatly; as stated, this refers to Petra, which is located in modern Jordan),* **where she is nourished for a time, and times, and half a time, from the face of the serpent** *(refers to three and one half years, the last half of the Great Tribulation; the Antichrist will take his armies elsewhere, thinking to take care of this remnant a little later [Dan. 11:44]).*

"**And the serpent cast out of his mouth water as a flood after the woman** *(refers to the army of the Antichrist, which* *has just defeated Israel and is now bent on completely destroying her),* **that he might cause her to be carried away of the flood.** *(The man of sin fully intends to destroy Israel at this time, but the Lord will intervene to stop him, as the next Verse proclaims.)"*

AN EARTHQUAKE?

"And the earth helped the woman *(probably refers to the Lord sending an earthquake),* **and the earth opened her mouth, and swallowed up the flood which the dragon cast out of his mouth.** *(This proclaims the action that helps the woman [Israel] hurts the dragon. As stated, it will probably be an earthquake!)*

"And the dragon was wroth with the woman *(Israel has escaped out of the clutches of Satan one more time),* **and went to make war with the Remnant of her seed** *(after the Rapture of the 144,000 Jews, with their Testimony still ringing out over Israel, no doubt, many other Jews will accept Christ at that time and make up the 'Remnant'),* **who keep the Commandments of God, and have the Testimony of Jesus Christ.** *(As stated, this refers to the fact that this Remnant of Jews, ever how many there will be, will have accepted Christ, hence, greatly angering Satan)"* **(Rev. 12:13-17).**

TIDINGS OUT OF THE EAST AND
OUT OF THE NORTH

The Antichrist could easily destroy Israel at that particular time, but he will hear *"tidings out of the east and out of the north,"* which will greatly trouble him. He will have to leave Israel for the time being and take care of this pressing business. Exactly as to who the *"east"* and the *"north"* are, we aren't told. It could very well be China and Russia. In addressing this, Daniel said:

"But tidings out of the east and out of the north shall trouble him: therefore he shall go forth with a great fury to destroy, and utterly to make away many" (Dan. 11:44).

Incidentally, as an aside, Daniel 11:44 proclaims the fact that the Antichrist will not rule the entirety of the world. To be sure, that will be his goal, and, no doubt, he would succeed in that but for the Second Coming. But here in the last half of the Great Tribulation, he will spend nearly three and a half years attending to this situation out of the east and out of the north. For it to take that long, this tells us that the situation is not merely a skirmish but, in fact, huge battles. He will win those battles and then will come down against Israel in what we now know as the Battle of Armageddon.

THE INVASION OF ISRAEL

Concerning this very thing, the great Prophet Ezekiel said, *"After many days you shall be visited: in the latter years you shall come into the land that is brought back from the sword, and is gathered out of many people, against the mountains of Israel, which have been always waste: but is brought forth out of the nations, and they shall dwell safely all of them"* (Ezek. 38:8).

"Armageddon" refers to the place where the actual Battle will begin, even though it will ultimately cover all of Israel. Armageddon can be defined as the Mount of Megiddo, which overlooks the Plain of Megiddo west of the Mount, and apparently including the Plain of Esdraelon, i.e., Valley of Megiddo. The area is also referred to as the *"Valley of Jehoshaphat."*

I have personally driven the length of this valley. Before Israel became a Nation, it was basically swamp and used for nothing. Not long after becoming a Nation in 1948, Israel began to drain that swamp, and now crops are grown there 12 months out of the year.

While the Battle could very well begin there, because it is an excellent area for tank warfare, it will not remain there, actually covering the majority of the Country of Israel and, especially, Jerusalem.

Megiddo, or Armageddon, has been the scene of many battles for many centuries, but this will be, as should be obvious, the greatest battle of them all. This is where and when Satan makes his biggest play. As we've already stated, if he can defeat Israel, then all the hundreds of Prophecies and Predictions by the Patriarchs and Prophets of old will fall to the ground. If, in fact, that happens, this means that Satan is now the god of the Universe. Of course, we know that it will not happen. Instead of Armageddon being his worldwide victory for all the world to see, it, in fact, will be his death and his doom. There, even as we shall see, he will find out as to exactly Who Jesus Christ really is and as to exactly What Jesus Christ can do. Instead of a victory, it will be a funeral—his.

CHAPTER SIX

PARTICIPANTS IN THE BATTLE

We will deal with Israel first.

There is no evidence that anyone in the world at that time, even America, will stand up for Israel. In other words, they will be facing the most powerful army, more than likely, the world has ever known and will do so alone. There is no indication in the Bible, of which I am aware, that speaks of any nation in the world helping Israel at that time. It will be somewhat like the situation was at the outset of World War II. Ships loaded with tens of thousands of Jewish refugees sailed from Europe and tried to find harbor in New York City. President Roosevelt would not allow them to disembark. His reason, *"It might antagonize Herr Hitler."* Some of the same ships went down to South America but, again, to no avail. They concluded their journey by going back to Europe, with most of those Jews gassed to death in the concentration camps. Among other things, it is no doubt, Hitler reasoned that no one cared if Jews lived or died, so he could take his freedom in slaughtering as many as he could find, and that's exactly what he did.

That's at least one of the reasons that America, plus most other nations of the world, had a guilty conscience after World

War II. America knew that she could have exerted some pressure on Hitler, which would have lessened the blow, but the upshot was, nothing was done.

In the coming Great Tribulation, likewise, the greater majority, if not all the nations of the world, will have no desire to antagonize the man of sin. The evidence is that even those who will consider themselves to be neutral will not lift a hand to help Israel so as not to bring the wrath of the Antichrist upon their heads. It must be remembered, at that particular time, at least, for the first few days, it will look as though the Antichrist is going to accomplish what Haman, Herod, and Hitler did not do. It will look like he is going to annihilate every Jew, which means a wholesale massacre. So, Israel will fight alone.

And yet, despite being outnumbered, possibly hundreds to one, the great Prophet Zechariah did say the following:

"In that day shall the LORD defend the inhabitants of Jerusalem; and he who is feeble among them at that day shall be as David; and the House of David shall be as God, as the Angel of the LORD before them" (Zech. 12:8).

THE ANOINTING OF POWER

The idea of all of this is, even though the army of Israel will, no doubt, be outnumbered greatly so by the army of the Antichrist, still, the Lord will make the Israeli soldiers as David of old, meaning that one will have the strength of 10 men or more. And then, the Tribe of Judah will have the unexcelled Power of God. But still, even though this supernatural ability given to the Jewish soldiers by the Lord will help greatly, that alone will not see them through because of the overwhelming superiority of the army of the Antichrist.

But, as one might say, as that which the Lord will do will be so very, very helpful, still, it is not the main entrée. The main entrée will be the Second Coming of the Lord, which we will deal with later.

THE ARMY OF THE ANTICHRIST

While the Bible gives us a few clues as to what this army will be made of, I'm sure it is only scratching the surface. No doubt, every nation conquered by the Antichrist will be forced to supply as many soldiers as the man of sin says are needed.

The Bible does give us a clue about at least some of those who will be with the man of sin.

The first one is *"Persia."* This, of course, is Iran. Many people do not know that Iran is not Arab, but rather Persian. Its history goes back some 2,500 years ago. The Iranians now, as is obvious, are rabid haters of Israel, swearing her destruction time and time again. In fact, Israel, at this present time, is on the horns of a dilemma. They have the power to take out Iran, but it would entail the slaughter of tens of thousands of Iranians, which the world would not sanction. At the same time, America, sadly and regrettably, is not doing anything about the proliferation of atomic power regarding Iran, which is working feverishly to develop its own atomic arsenal. Strangely enough, the surrounding Arab nations wish that Israel would do something simply because Iran hates them almost as much as they hate Israel. So, Israel is attempting to slow down, if not halt, the atomic development in Iran by taking out, in various different ways, her top scientists, etc. Israel is fastly finding herself with precious few friends. That's the reason that when the Antichrist makes his debut, claiming to be able to solve the problem between Israel and the Muslims, and, in fact, will do so, this will be the greatest thing in the eyes of the world that has happened in the last several decades.

Israel also listed the following countries:

• Ethiopia: this is a small country located on the eastern side of the middle part of the Continent of Africa. About all they could contribute to the army of the Antichrist would be soldiers, but yet, of little consequence.

• Libya: this little country is in northern Africa and, as well, can supply precious little in the form of military help.

If it is to be noticed, when the Bible mentions weapons of war, it mentions that which is indicative of that particular time, such as the *"sword, bucklers and shields."* However, that doesn't mean that this Battle will be fought with weapons of antiquity. Far from it! In fact, the Antichrist, no doubt, will have the finest weaponry in the world. And yet, it is doubtful that he will have atomic bombs.

It should be obvious, if the sacred writers had used the names of modern weapons, Bible scholars for many centuries would have been deeply puzzled, not understanding at all what the names of the weapons would have meant. So, the weapons of that time were rightly listed. However, make no mistake about it, the weapons that will be used in the coming Great Tribulation will be the very finest available.

• Gomer: there is some small evidence that these people came from the Ukraine, which was a part of the Soviet Union when Communism was in power. It now has its own sovereignty. Some have claimed that Gomer referred to Germany; however, there is really no proof of that.

• Togarmah: some think these people may have come from what is now Iraq, but again, that is only speculative.

AT THE TIME OF THE BATTLE OF ARMAGEDDON, WHAT PART WILL MUSLIMS PLAY?

We have already alluded to the following but allow me to elaborate. While, no doubt, great promises will be made to the Muslims at the beginning of the Great Tribulation, the hour will come that the man of sin will set himself up as God. This will be at about the midpoint of the seven-year period. So, the promises he will have made to the Muslims at the outset, that is, if he, in fact, does make promises, will, no doubt, be completely ignored.

From the way Daniel describes the Antichrist, he cannot tolerate and, in fact, will not tolerate any competing religion of any kind. He will claim to be God, so that doesn't leave any room for competing religions such as Islam, etc.

However, the age-old hatred of the Muslims against Israel will most definitely not change. So, even though he will not do for the Muslims what possibly he will promise to do, still, his hatred for Israel will be paramount. Quite possibly, they will take whatever they can get that, hopefully, will destroy the ancient people.

It is my personal thought that this man will, in fact, take over the entirety of the Middle East with all of its oil, which will shut the Muslims out. I also believe that he will do away with the worshipping spot of Mecca. At a point in time, realizing what he is doing, they will then, no doubt, try to salvage any place for themselves that they can get. At any rate, during that time, the religion of Islam, plus all other religions, will be no more, at least, in the countries where he has control. So, after he finishes the countries *"out of the east and out of the north,"* which, as stated, could very well be Russia and China, he will then turn his attention to Israel. They will be the only people on the face of the Earth of that time, of which we have any knowledge, who will oppose the Antichrist.

The man of sin will turn on Israel at the midpoint of the Great Tribulation, with Israel then fleeing to Petra, which is in Jordan. He will hear these evil tidings out of the east and out of the north and will leave Israel and will set about to take care of this pressing problem. With the Antichrist having moved his vast army, Israel will begin to filter back into Jerusalem, at least all of its men, and many of its young ladies as well. They will then begin to rearm themselves and will have about three years to do so. So, at the time of the Battle of Armageddon, Israel, with her meager forces, will face this juggernaut alone.

WHERE WILL AMERICA BE DURING THIS TIME?

One must understand that with the Rapture (Resurrection) of the Church, that which made America great, and I speak of the hundreds of thousands, or even millions, of Born-Again Believers, will no longer be here. While, no doubt, hundreds of thousands will give their hearts to Christ immediately after the Rapture, still, America will not be the place that we now know. The spirit of the Antichrist is already at work in America and, in fact, in the entirety of the world; however, I think it is at work in America greater than anywhere else.

The reason I feel this is because the United States is still the center for world Evangelism, and, of course, Satan will go to any length to stop that. I personally believe that the Lord, for the time being, is going to hold everything in check so that this great *"Message of the Cross"* will not only cover this great nation but, also, every other nation in the world. To be sure, the Lord places great stock in His Word going to the world and, especially, the MESSAGE OF THE CROSS.

While there is no evidence that the Antichrist will take over America during the Great Tribulation, still, there is no evidence, either, that America will oppose him. In fact, every evidence is that our nation will applaud him, at least, at the beginning, because of his being able to broker a peace treaty between Israel and the Muslims, something that the brightest minds in America have never been able to accomplish.

There will be many nations that will throw in with the Antichrist, thereby, giving him their full support, but only because they have no choice. Every evidence is that, at the outset, he will take over the entirety of the Middle East, with the exception of Jordan and much of Western Europe.

WHAT ABOUT THE TEN-NATION CONFEDERATION?

The Word of God has quite a bit to say about this ten-nation confederation, which goes all the way back to the dream given to Nebuchadnezzar, the golden head, so to speak, of the Babylonian Empire. This was done some 2,500 years ago.

Ironically enough, this potentate couldn't even remember what the dream was, much less, its interpretation. Of course, the Lord orchestrated all of this. Daniel would recall the dream and, as well, give him the interpretation. As we shall see, the dream and its interpretation portray to us all the empires that would persecute Israel from the time of the Babylonians even unto the future, which means it has not yet come to pass. In fact, all of the empires have come and gone, with the exception of the ten-nation confederation, which is right around the corner, so to speak.

Concerning this ten-nation confederation, the Word of God says:

"And the fourth kingdom shall be strong as iron: forasmuch as iron breaks in pieces and subdues all things: and as iron that breaks all these, shall it break in pieces and bruise. *(This 'fourth kingdom' is the Roman Empire and is represented by the 'legs of iron.' It would be the strongest of all!)*

"And whereas you saw the feet and toes, part of the potters' clay, and part of iron, the kingdom shall be divided; but there shall be in it of the strength of the iron, forasmuch as you saw the iron mixed with miry clay. *(All that we have previously studied represents empires that have come and gone; however, the 'feet' and 'toes' of this statue of iron and clay represent that which is yet to come.)*

"And as the toes of the feet were part of iron, and part of clay, so the kingdom shall be partly strong, and partly broken. *(This Verse represents the ten-nation confederation, with the 'toes of the feet' symbolic of this confederation, which will greatly oppose Israel in the very near future.)*

"And whereas you saw iron mixed with miry clay, they shall mingle themselves with the seed of men: but they shall not cleave one to another, even as iron is not mixed with clay. *(Their confederation will not succeed because of the 'miry clay,' which expresses that some of the ten-nation confederation are weak. As stated, this will take place in the near future)*" **(Dan. 2:40-43).**

THE ROMAN EMPIRE AND THE TEN-NATION KINGDOM

"After this I saw in the night Visions, and behold a

fourth beast, dreadful and terrible, and strong exceedingly; and it had great iron teeth: it devoured and broke in pieces, and stamped the residue with the feet of it: and it was diverse from all the beasts that were before it; and it had ten horns. *(This beast represents the Roman Empire, which was the strongest and most powerful of all. It lasted for nearly 1,000 years.*

"The phrase, 'And it had ten horns,' speaks of that which was a part of this beast, and for a particular reason. But it had nothing to do with the conquests of the original Roman Empire. These 'ten horns' portray ten kingdoms, which will arise in the latter days, in fact, in the very near future. These ten nations will persecute Israel)" **(Dan. 7:7).**

Even though we have already given the following in this Volume, for clarification, please allow the repetition, inasmuch as it involves the ten-nation confederation.

THE LITTLE HORN

"I considered the horns, and, behold, there came up among them another little horn, before whom there were three of the first horns plucked up by the roots: and, behold, in this horn were eyes like the eyes of a man, and a mouth speaking great things. *(At first, Daniel did not understand the horns. Even though the Roman Empire has come and gone, still, the 'ten horns' have not yet risen to power; however, the breakup of the former Soviet Union is the beginning of the fulfillment of this Passage. If one is to notice, the 'ten horns' were a part of the non-descript beast, which has to do with the territory which the old Roman Empire controlled.*

"'There came up among them another little horn,' means this one came up after the 'ten horns' were fully grown. The 'little horn' is the Antichrist.

"Three of the horns will be plucked by the 'little horn,'

*meaning that he will defeat these countries in battle, with
the others then submitting to him. This will take place in
the first half of the Great Tribulation)"* **(Dan. 7:8).**

The three horns, i.e., three nations that will be defeated by
the Antichrist, are Egypt, Turkey, and Greece. We know these
are the countries addressed because of the location of Alexander
the Great's Empire, and the way it was broken up and taken
over by his four generals.

KING OF THE SOUTH

Daniel said, *"And at the time of the end shall the king of
the south push at him: and the king of the north shall come
against him like a whirlwind, with chariots, and with horsemen,
and with many ships; and he shall enter into the countries, and
shall overflow and pass over"* (Dan. 11:40).

The phrase, *"Shall the king of the south push at him,"*
refers to Egypt attacking the Antichrist. In fact, Egypt will
head up the ten-nation confederation, corresponding with the
"ten horns" of Daniel 7:7, which will greatly oppose Israel. We
know that the *"king of the south"* refers to Egypt because this
is who is referred to at the beginning of this Eleventh Chapter
of Daniel, which speaks of the breakup of the Grecian Empire
with the death of Alexander the Great.

It seems that Greece and Turkey will join with Egypt in
attempting to stop the *"king of the north,"* who will be the
Antichrist. We know that these are the two countries referred
to (Greece and Turkey) from Daniel 8:9. As is obvious, they
will not at all be successful and will quickly be defeated by the
man of sin, with the other six countries throwing in their lot
with him without further conflict. In other words, they will
realize that opposing him is futile.

With the Antichrist getting control over the three countries
mentioned in the first three and a half years of Daniel's seventieth
week, and the other six giving their power to him upon seeing

further resistance as useless, this makes him the conqueror of all the old Roman Empire territory. Therefore, his base of operations at the midway point of the Great Tribulation will be substantial, to say the least!

Regarding the ten countries fulfilling the *"ten horns"* of Daniel 7:7, the Antichrist will already be the ruler over Syria, and with him defeating three, that leaves only six. These will give their power to him, giving him control of all 10.

Who the six countries are, we aren't told, but, for certain, they will be with him when he turns on Israel.

CHAPTER SEVEN

THE REPENTANCE OF ISRAEL

At this juncture, I think it would be good to briefly address ourselves to Israel's Repentance, at least, after a sort. This prayer will, no doubt, be prayed, in one form or the other, immediately before the Second Coming. It was given by Isaiah nearly 2,800 years ago. It could well be that they will come to this place that Isaiah portrays in the closing hours of Armageddon. At that time, and beyond the shadow of a doubt, Israel will know that the coming of the True Messiah is their only hope. It is that or total destruction. Now we will see how the Holy Spirit gave the hearts' cry of these ancient people to the great Prophet Isaiah nearly 2,800 years ago. He said:

PRAYER FOR DELIVERANCE

"Look down from Heaven, and behold from the habitation of Your Holiness and of Your Glory: where is Your Zeal and Your Strength, the sounding of Your Bowels and of Your Mercies toward me? are they restrained? *(This prayer, in effect, will be prayed by Israel, as stated, or rather the Believing Remnant of Israel, prior to the*

Second Coming.

"The Faith, attachment, and anguish of the prayer are most effecting, and are made the more so by the way in which the Holy Spirit lends Himself to the feelings of a dependent and desolate heart, recalling past blessings, expressing present distress, acknowledging sin and the justice of God's Judicial Blinding, but pleading for Deliverance, not because of the Repentance and Faith of the supplicants, but nevertheless required, but because of the election of God and the immutability of His Nature)" **(Isa. 63:15).**

YOU ARE OUR FATHER

"Doubtless You are our Father, though Abraham be ignorant of us, and Israel acknowledge us not: You, O LORD, are our Father, our Redeemer; Your Name is from everlasting. *(The Pharisee based his expectation of Salvation upon his relationship to Abraham, but the spiritual Israelite bases his upon his relationship to God. When facing Christ at His First Advent, they boasted that they were children of Abraham [Jn. 8:39]. Now at the eve of His Second Advent, they boast no more, but rather confess that Abraham would not even own them, i.e., 'be ignorant of us.'*

"They now admit that Israel, i.e., Jacob, would not even 'acknowledge them.'

" 'Doubtless You are our Father,' rather says, 'If You will not be our Father, then we have no Father!' This is the ground of their appeal to God. They acknowledge that their ancient relationship to Abraham and Jacob cannot redeem them. If the Lord does not claim them and redeem them, they are eternally lost!)" **(Isa. 63:16).**

A JUDICIAL JUDGMENT

"O LORD, why have You made us to err from Your Ways, and hardened our heart from Your Fear?

Return for Your Servants' sake, the tribes of Your Inheritance. *(Verse 17 should read: 'O Jehovah, why have You suffered us to err from Your Ways? And why have You let us harden our hearts to Your Fear?' Thus, true Repentance confesses that God justly gives men over to a hardened heart when they resist His Will. At the same time, Faith holds to it that the Tribes of Jacob were God's Inheritance and His Holy People.*

" 'Hardened our heart from Your Fear,' refers to the fact that when men have scornfully and obstinately rejected the Grace of God, God withdraws it from them judicially, giving them up to their wanderings, which makes their hearts incapable of Faith.

" 'Return for Your Servants' sake,' speaks of humility and no longer of a hardened heart)" **(Isa. 63:17).**

OUR ADVERSARIES HAVE TRODDEN DOWN YOUR SANCTUARY

"The people of Your Holiness have possessed it but a little while: our adversaries have trodden down Your Sanctuary. *(The great 'inheritance' that God gave unto His People was 'possessed by them only a little while.' As a result of their sin, 'our adversaries have trodden down Your Sanctuary.' They are referring to the destruction by Nebuchadnezzar and by Titus, the Roman General. But more than all, they are speaking of the Antichrist, whom they erroneously thought was the Messiah, but who turned on them and did 'trod down their Sanctuary' [Dan. 9:27])"* **(Isa. 63:18).**

WE ARE YOURS

"We are Yours: You never bore rule over them; they were not called by Your Name. *(There is no 'Thine' [Yours] in the original, and so important a word could not possibly* *be supplied from without. Therefore, the translation should read, 'We are as those over whom You have not ruled from of old, as those upon whom Your Name has not been called; i.e., we have lost all our privileges – we have become in God's Sight no better than the heathen – He has forgotten that we were ever His People)"* **(Isa. 63:19).**

CONFESSION OF SIN

"But we are all as an unclean thing, and all our righteousnesses are as filthy rags; and we all do fade as a leaf; and our iniquities, like the wind, have taken us away. *(Here Israel confesses the reason for their desperate condition. At long last, they own up as to exactly what it is, 'our iniquities.'*

" 'But we are all as an unclean thing,' is actually saying before God that they are a spiritual leper. They now recognize that their self-righteousness is no more than 'filthy rags,' which refer to the menstrual flux of a woman regarding her monthly period.

"It is very difficult for men, and especially religious men, to admit to such! Hence, not many religious men are Saved!)" **(Isa. 64:6).**

OUR INIQUITIES

"And there is none who calls upon Your Name, who stirs up himself to take hold of You: for You have hid Your Face from us, and have consumed us, because of our iniquities. *(Once again, Israel admits that it is her 'iniquities', which have brought about the judgment of God upon her. She has only herself to blame!)"* **(Isa. 64:7).**

The phrase, *"There is none who calls upon Your Name,"* is hyperbole, similar to: *"There is none who does good, no, not one"* (Ps. 14:3).

Because of Israel's great sins, a general lethargy and apathy had come over the people so that they could but with difficulty rouse themselves to Faith and calling upon God. Even then, there was a small *"Remnant,"* which *"prayed and did not faint."* However, this number was always few.

The phrase, *"Who stirs up himself to take hold of You,"* expresses more than mere prayer; it is earnest, intense, *"effectual, fervent"* prayer. The implication from the words, *"stirs up himself,"* speaks of an individual forging ahead without much encouragement from others.

The phrase, *"Take hold of You,"* referring to taking hold of the Lord, means *"to fasten upon, seize, be strong, courageous, obstinate, to bind, restrain, conquer, catch, cleave to, be constant, continue, force, lay hold on, maintain, wax mighty, prevail, be urgent, wax strong."*

Anyone who follows such a course is guaranteed to find the Lord as well as an answer to petition and prayer.

"For You have hid Your Face from us," speaks of God no longer looking on the individuals with favor. The phrase, *"And have consumed us, because of our iniquities,"* refers to being delivered unto the power of destruction because of sin. Men's sins are their master; they exercise a tyrannical control over them, which they often are quite unable to resist (Ezek. 33:10). At times, God judicially delivers the wicked into the power of their sins (Rom. 1:24-28). In other words, if men will to sin, God wills more sin unto them.

Sin is not just an act, an infraction, or the breaking of a rule or law. It is far more than that, actually, a spirit that seizes man to the extent that he is unable, within his own power, to shake it off. Hence, the idea that psychological counseling, or any other foolish man-devised method, can assuage such power is foolishness indeed! Only the Power of God can set the captive free and release the prisoner from the prison house.

YOU ARE THE POTTER, WE ARE THE CLAY

"But now, O LORD, You are our Father; we are the

clay, and You our Potter; and we all are the Work of Your Hand. *(In this Passage is the gist of the great Salvation Message of Christianity. Only God can change the shape of the clay, thereby, molding the vessel into the shape and design that is desired, thereby, mending the flaws and weaknesses)"* (Isa. 64:8).

The heavenly *"Potter"* will not forcibly take control, irrespective of the desperation of the *"clay."* That control must be freely given and longingly desired before the Heavenly Father will mold our lives into His Image (Rom. 8:29; I Cor. 15:49).

Paul said, *"And have put on the new man, which is renewed in knowledge after the Image of Him Who created him"* (Col. 3:10).

The church must realize that such cannot be *"the Work of Your Hand"* and the work of man's hand at the same time!

LORD, NEITHER REMEMBER INIQUITY FOREVER

"Be not wroth very sore, O LORD, neither remember iniquity forever: behold, see, we beseech You, we are all Your People. *(The appeal here is for God to begin all over again, like the potter with the clay. The idea of the phrase, 'Be not wroth very sore,' refers to the fact that God had become very angry with His People. The reason for that anger was sin on the part of Israel. God cannot abide sin in the lives of His Own People any more than He can in the wicked)"* (Isa. 64:9).

The phrase, *"Neither remember iniquity forever,"* proclaims the fact that whenever the Lord cleanses sin, He also forgets the sin.

Down through the years, many have asked the question, *"Can a homosexual, or some other such type of individual, be Saved?"*

The answer is Biblically clear (Jn. 3:16). Anyone who comes to the Lord, confessing the Lord with his mouth and believing in his heart that God has raised Christ from the dead, that person will be Saved (Rom. 10:9-10, 13). So, the record is clear. The Lord will save anyone who sincerely comes to Him.

However, it should be noted that the Lord does not save such *"in"* their sin but *"from"* their sin! In other words, the homosexual, the alcoholic, the drug addict, the liar, the thief, etc., once Born-Again, are no longer what they once were. They cease the previous activity. The homosexual quits practicing that sin, which goes for all other types of sins and sinners as well.

The overwhelming power of Biblical Christianity is that it changes men. The idea that the only difference between the Believer and the unbeliever is the Blood of Christ is specious indeed! The very nature of the Born-Again experience is that it changes people. Actually, that is its very purpose.

The Blood of Christ, God's Son, cleanses and washes the sinner, and the Power of God, through the Holy Spirit, changes the sinner.

"Therefore if any man be in Christ, he is a new creation: old things are passed away; behold, all things are become new" (II Cor. 5:17).

In Verse 9, Israel, on that morning when she will repent before God, requests that her many sins be remembered no more. They are admitting that they have sinned, and sinned miserably. So, the fact of their sin is not in question. This, they acknowledge, but they also reverently request that God *"neither remember iniquity forever."* In this prayer, they demand nothing—they only *"beseech,"* or *"beg."*

The Lord had already made a Promise by the mouth of Isaiah, *"I, even I, am He Who blots out your transgressions for My Own Sake, and will not remember your sins"* (Isa. 43:25). Israel now lays hold of this Promise and entreats that their *"iniquity"* may not only be forgiven but also forgotten.

GOD'S PEOPLE

The phrase, *"Behold, see, we beseech You, we are all Your People,"* claims God as their Father. This is a fresh argument.

They are saying, *"We are Your Work, Your Creatures,"* speaking of such in an individual sense. It also speaks collectively.

The words, *"Your People,"* refer to the people whom God had chosen to Himself, and over whom He had watched for so many centuries. In other words, He had lavished labor and skill upon them. Surely, He would not *"forsake the Work of His Own Hands"* (Ps. 138:8).

This is a prayer of true Repentance, a prayer, which, incidentally, will be prayed immediately before the Second Coming and, no doubt, even after the Second Coming. Any person who prays this type of prayer and is sincere in his heart, God will forgive, cleanse, wash, and forget all that was done in the past. He has promised to do so, and He cannot lie!

BESEECHING THE LORD

"Your holy cities are a wilderness, Zion is a wilderness, Jerusalem a desolation. *(As we have stated, the entirety of this prayer of Repentance, which began in the Fifteenth Verse of the previous Chapter, will be prayed by Israel at the end of the Great Tribulation – at the Second Advent of Christ, which, in fact, will precipitate His Coming)"* (Isa. 64:10).

When Jesus comes back the Second Time, Israel, as would be obvious, will be in ruins. Jerusalem will be totally wrecked. The description of *"wilderness"* and *"desolation"* presents an apt summation of the situation.

In effect, Israel is saying to the Lord, *"It is our sin that has done this. You Alone can remedy our condition."* And remedy it, He will!

LAID WASTE

"Our Holy and our beautiful House, where our fathers praised You, is burned up with fire: and all our pleasant things are laid waste. *(This speaks of the Temple that is yet to be built in Jerusalem. In fact, when the Antichrist turns on Israel, he will make their Temple his religious headquarters, committing every act of vileness that one could think)"* **(Isa. 64:11).**

The truth is, even though this Temple, which will be built in the coming Great Tribulation, will be for the worship of God, it is worship that He will not accept. In fact, Israel will begin the Sacrificial system, which hasn't been carried out for some 2,000 years, but the following is what the Word of God says about that matter:

"And there was given me a reed like unto a rod: and the Angel stood, saying, Rise, and measure the Temple of God, and the Altar, and them who worship therein" (Rev. 11:1).

Under such circumstances, whenever a measurement is carried out and given, it is always for Judgment.

Jesus Christ fulfilled the entirety of the Mosaic Law, which means that Temple worship is no longer necessary, nor, in the Mind of God, is it allowed. The rebuilding of the Temple, which will be done by Israel most likely during the first half of the Great Tribulation, will, in essence, say that Jesus Christ was an imposter and that the Mosaic Law is still in vogue. The Lord cannot tolerate that.

In fact, the Early Church had great problems with this. The Jewish segment in Jerusalem continued to try to keep the Law and to engage in Temple worship, despite what the Lord had given to the Apostle Paul concerning the Lord fulfilling all of this by His Life, Death, and Resurrection. In effect, the Lord grew so sick of this, and I continue to speak of Temple worship, that He used the Roman General, Titus, to completely demolish the Temple, fulfilling the Words of Christ in totality (Mat. 24:1-2).

In fact, Israel will be able to build her Temple as the result of claiming that the Antichrist is her Messiah, etc. So, Israel's position and condition then will be far different than at the conclusion of the Great Tribulation. By that time, they will realize they have played the fool, and the one they thought was their

Messiah actually hates them and is doing everything within his power to destroy them. As the Battle of Armageddon rages, for a period of time, it will look like he will succeed, but the Second Coming will turn everything around, including Israel.

LORD, WILL YOU NOT HELP US?

"Will You refrain Yourself for these things, O LORD? will You hold Your Peace, and afflict us very sore? *(Israel first repents of her terrible sins, pleading God's Mercy, Grace, and Love. They then bring to His Attention the terrible plight of the 'holy cities' and of 'Jerusalem.' Last of all, they proclaim to Him the destruction of the Temple.*
"They then ask, 'Will You refrain Yourself for these things, O LORD?'
"The answer is certain. He will not refrain Himself! He will not hold His Peace!)" **(Isa. 64:12).**

This prayer, prayed at Israel's most desperate moment, when it looks like the Antichrist will take the day and will completely annihilate them, shows a repentant heart, and it will bring back the Lord Jesus Christ. Admittedly, in this prayer, they do not acknowledge Jesus Christ because, as of yet, they still do not believe in Jesus Christ. However, that will change immediately at the Second Coming.

But yet, their prayer of Repentance does show a broken heart and a contrite spirit, which the Lord will answer and, in fact, will ever answer. The matter of the Lord Jesus Christ, which, of course, is the greatest matter of all, will be handled, as stated, immediately at the Second Coming. Then they will know Who their Messiah really is, which will precipitate a mourning all over the land of Israel, and rightly so. In other words, the mourning will have to do with the terrible sin they committed in crucifying the Lord. They will then realize what a horrible mistake they made, and how they have suffered so very, very much for that mistake. But to be sure, the Lord will most definitely forgive (Zech. 12:11-14).

CHAPTER EIGHT

THE BATTLE OF ARMAGEDDON

We are given very little Scriptural information about Daniel, Chapter 11, Verse 44, where tidings out of the east and the north will cause the Antichrist great problems. From what little we are told, it is obvious that something big will happen at that time. Actually, it will take place at approximately the midpoint of the Great Tribulation, causing the man of sin to leave off of Israel and take care of these pressing problems.

We are not given the names of the countries that are giving him problems, only that they are *"out of the east and out of the north."* That means north of Israel and east of Israel. It will not involve the countries in the Middle East because they are already under his domain at that time. So, more than likely, it will be Russia and China, for these are the only two countries that have a military of any significance. Irrespective, it said that these countries *"shall trouble him."*

Exactly what that means, we aren't told. However, it could very well mean that they now see what this man is all about, which is to take over the entirety of the world. Ever how it is done, or ever what is done, they will oppose him. Whatever it is that they do, it will cause him to respond *"with great fury to destroy, and utterly to make away many."* Evidently, he sees them as attempting to stand in his way regarding his ambition as world conqueror.

As well, the indication is that this is not something small due to the fact that, as far as we know, it is going to take all of the latter half of the Great Tribulation. In other words, it will take about three and a half years for him to put down this opposition; however, he will put it down and will come out of the conflict stronger than ever. But now, he must take care of Israel.

SATAN AND ISRAEL

We've already addressed this subject in this Volume, and I speak of the hatred for Israel, but allow me to repeat myself. This hatred exists simply because of God's Plan for these ancient people, His People, I might quickly add, as well as Satan's plan. The consuming effort to destroy Israel, which characterized the Holocaust and every other similar effort, stems from the fact that Satan knows that if he can annihilate every Jew and take over the Nation called *"Israel,"* this will abrogate the Word of God. That means that it will fall to the ground and Satan wins. The Word of God is sacrosanct in every capacity. Considering that there are more Predictions, more Prophecies, and more Promises in the Word of God concerning the Restoration of Israel than anything else, this is why Satan has set out to destroy them.

The Jewish people, of course, understand the hatred simply because this thing didn't start yesterday; it began thousands of years ago. Read carefully what the great Prophet Jeremiah said as it regards this very thing:

"My Heritage is unto Me as a speckled bird, the birds round about are against her; come you, assemble all the beasts of the field, come to devour" (Jer. 12:9).

If it is to be noticed, the Holy Spirit through the Prophet said, *"The birds round about are against her."* This spoke of the nations around Israel that were opposed to her, actually, that opposition never ceased. In fact, the same animosity is registered against true Christians. It is because the God of the Bible is Real, Jesus Christ, God's Only Son, is Real, the Word of God is Real, and those who follow the Lord are real as well. At the same time, it means that every other religion in the world is not real, which means that they are of the Devil. That is blunt but true.

When President Bush was in London, the English press asked him if he believed that Christians and Muslims pray to the same God, and he answered, *"Yes."* He could not have been more wrong. Allah is not God. As we've already stated in this Volume, Muhammad selected this name out of the scores of names of so-called Babylonian deities. Regrettably, many Christians have the erroneous idea that Jehovah and Allah are one and the same. To be frank, such is blasphemy! So, the hatred that will fill the Antichrist against Israel will be placed there by Satan himself, and now comes Satan's fell swoop, so to speak. What Haman, Herod, and Hitler could not do, the man of sin will now accomplish. He will totally and completely annihilate every Jew in Israel, and after that is done, and he confiscates their land, he will then demand the death of every other Jew on the face of the Earth. Considering how strong that he will be, no one will be able to resist him.

THE SIGNIFICANCE OF ARMAGEDDON

As we've already stated, this Battle is designed to completely destroy Israel; however, it is also designed for a far more important reason. It is for the Evil One, Satan himself, to become the god of the Universe. Of course, this thing did not start yesterday, and neither will Armageddon be its beginning. It started at the very beginning of time. Let's look for a few moments at the efforts made by Satan to destroy Israel, which were to destroy the Plan of God on this Earth. These efforts will intensify, especially, in these last days.

To be sure, Satan's opposition against the Church is no less; however, because the Church of Jesus Christ is not a distinct state, as Israel, his opposition is somewhat different. Now he seeks to corrupt the Gospel, which he has been very successful in doing.

Concerning this hatred, John the Beloved wrote, and we quote:

THE GREAT WHORE

"And there came one of the seven Angels which had the seven Vials, and talked with me *(probably is the seventh Angel; however, we actually have no way of truly knowing)*, saying unto me, Come hither; I will show unto you the Judgment of the great whore who sits upon many waters *(the 'great whore' refers to all the religions of the world that ever have been, which are devised by men as a substitute for 'Jesus Christ and Him Crucified'; God's Way is Christ and Him Crucified Alone; as well, the 'many waters' are a symbol for multitudes of people [Vs. 15])*:

"With whom *(the great whore, i.e., all types of religions)* the kings of the Earth *(from the very beginning, most nations have been ruled by some type of religion)* have committed fornication *(all religions devised by men, and even the parts of Christianity that have been corrupted, are labeled by the Lord as 'spiritual fornication,' in other words, they look to something else other than the Lord [Rom. 7:1-4])*, and the inhabitants of the Earth have been made drunk with the wine of her fornication *(proclaims the addiction of religion; the doing of religion is the most powerful narcotic there is)*."

THE WOMAN

"So he *(the Angel)* carried me *(John)* away in the spirit *(a Vision)* into the wilderness *(every religious effort that attempts to take the place of the Cross is a spiritual wilderness)*: and I saw a woman sit upon a scarlet coloured

beast *(the woman is organized religion; by that we mean any religion or form of religion claiming to have a way of Salvation or victory other than the Cross; the 'scarlet color' indicates blood and pertains to great persecution)*, **full of names of blasphemy** *(refers to this 'woman' opposing the Plan of God in every capacity)*, **having seven heads and ten horns.** *(This pertains to the scarlet colored beast, not the woman. The 'seven heads' represent seven empires that persecuted Israel in the past, with the last one yet future. They are 'Egypt, Assyria, Babylon, Medo-Persia, Greece and Rome.' The 'ten horns' represent ten nations that will arise out of the old Roman Empire territory and persecute Israel, and is yet future. These ten nations make up the seventh head. The Roman Empire, which made up the sixth head, was the last of the empires that persecuted Israel before her destruction as a Nation in A.D. 70. When the ten-horned kingdom arises, which it will shortly, it will persecute Israel as well.)*"

MYSTERY BABYLON THE GREAT

"**And the woman was arrayed in purple and scarlet colour** *(all of this pertains to Israel, but with a carry-over into the Church Age; the 'purple' represents the dominion of these religions over nations, with the 'scarlet color' representing the persecution of Israel)*, **and decked with gold and precious stones and pearls** *(these religions have always been very rich; a case in point is Islam, which controls some sixty percent of the oil reserves of the world)*, **having a golden cup in her hand** *(all of these religions have an allurement, symbolized by the cup being golden)* **full of abominations and filthiness of her fornication** *(proclaims what this cup holds, despite its outward attractiveness)*:
"**And upon her forehead *was* a name written** *(the 'forehead' symbolizes the fact that all these religions are*

devised by man and not by God), **MYSTERY, BABYLON THE GREAT** *(the word 'mystery' separates spiritual Babylon from literal Babylon; it is 'great in the eyes of the world, but not in the Eyes of God')*, **THE MOTHER OF HARLOTS AND ABOMINATIONS OF THE EARTH.** *(This proclaims the actual content of this 'golden cup,' even though it looks wonderful on the outside. If it's not 'Jesus Christ and Him Crucified,' then it is labeled by the Lord as 'harlots and abominations.' Regrettably that includes much of modern Christianity as well.)"*

THE BLOOD OF THE SAINTS

"**And I saw the woman drunken with the blood of the Saints** *(refers to these empires and their false religions, which persecuted Israel during Old Testament times, actually, up to the time of Christ)*, **and with the blood of the martyrs of Jesus** *(points to the millions in the Church Age who gave their lives for the Cause of Christ; the Roman Empire began these persecutions of Christians and was followed by the Catholic Church)*: **and when I saw her, I wondered with great admiration** *(John is amazed at seeing all of this).*

"**And the Angel said unto me, Wherefore did you marvel?** *(The Angel knew John would marvel at the scene that unfolded before his eyes and would need an explanation.)* **I will tell you the mystery of the woman, and of the beast that carries her, which has the seven heads and ten horns.**"

THE BEAST

"**The beast who you saw was** *(represents a fallen Angel who helped the leaders of these empires of the past in their efforts to destroy Israel)*, **and is not** *(was not active during the time of John)*; **and shall ascend out of the bottomless pit** *(this powerful, fallen Angel was confined* to the bottomless pit about 2,300 years ago and remains there still, but will be released soon to help the Antichrist)*, **and go into perdition** *(means that after his escapade of helping the Antichrist on Earth, he will be consigned to the Lake of Fire [Rev. 20:10])*; **and they who dwell on the Earth shall wonder, whose names were not written in the Book of Life from the foundation of the world** *(presents the fact that all the unsaved people on Earth during the time of the Great Tribulation will be startled and amazed as they observe the Antichrist, who will do things no other man has ever done; this will be because this fallen Angel is helping him, but of which he is not aware)*, **when they behold the beast who was, and is not** *(was not functioning during John's day)*, **and yet is** *(will be released out of the bottomless pit to help the Antichrist).*"

WISDOM

"**And here *is* the mind which has wisdom** *(is the mind which knows and believes the Word of God).* **The seven heads are seven mountains, on which the woman sits** *(represents these seven empires, which were controlled by false religions, i.e., 'demon spirits').*

"**And there are seven kings** *(actually refers to the 'seven heads,' speaking of the leaders of these empires, whomever they may have been)*: **five are fallen** *(five of the empires were fallen during John's day; they are Egypt, Assyria, Babylon, Medo-Persia, and Greece)*, **and one is** *(refers to the Roman Empire, which was in existence during John's day, and could, therefore, be spoken of in the present tense)*, ***and* the other is not yet come** *(refers to the ten-nation confederation symbolized by the ten horns, which in John's day had not yet come and, in fact, has not come even yet)*; **and when he comes, he must continue a short space.** *(The 'ten horns' will be the seventh head and refers to ten nations that will arise shortly and persecute*

Israel, which will probably take place in the first half of the Great Tribulation, a time span of about three and one half years.)"

THE FALLEN ANGEL

"**And the beast** *(fallen Angel)* **that was, and is not, even he is the eighth** *(this fallen Angel will help the Antichrist and will head up the eighth empire to persecute Israel)*, **and is of the seven** *(refers to the fact that he helped all the empires of the past, with the exception of Rome, in their efforts to persecute Israel; but this fallen Angel gave the greatest help to Alexander the Great, who headed up the Grecian Empire; we know this because John, in his Vision, said, 'And the beast which I saw was like unto a leopard,' with that animal being one of the symbols of ancient Greece [Rev. 13:2; Dan. 7:6])*, **and goes into perdition** *(refers to the fact that irrespective of his power and plans, eternal Hell will be the due of this satanic prince; the same goes for Satan, the Antichrist, the False Prophet, every fallen Angel, every demon spirit, and, in fact, all the unredeemed who have ever lived)*."

THE TEN-NATION CONFEDERATION

"**And the ten horns which you saw are ten kings** *(Dan. 7:7)*, **which have received no kingdom as yet** *(refers to John's day)*; **but receive power as kings one hour with the beast.** *(These ten nations will come to power before the Antichrist, making up the seventh head. Then they will be taken over by the Antichrist, who is referred to by Daniel as the 'little horn' [Dan. 7:8]. The 'one hour' refers to the 'short space' this confederation of the ten kings and the Antichrist will hold together. It will last for approximately three and one half years and will be destroyed by the Second Coming of Christ [Dan. 2:34-35].)*"

WHAT THE TEN NATIONS WILL DO,
WHICH IS YET FUTURE

"**These have one mind** *(this ten-nation confederation, making up the seventh head, will all be in agreement respecting their joining with the Antichrist because they don't have the power to successfully oppose him. Incidentally, these nations are in existence today but will probably not be revealed until the first part of the Great Tribulation)*, **and shall give their power and strength unto the beast** *(refers to the Antichrist now coming to full power and making up the eighth kingdom as described in Rev. 17:11)*.

"**These shall make war with the Lamb** *(has to do with the Antichrist attacking Israel as it regards the Battle of Armageddon; Satan hates Israel for many and varied reasons, but, above all, because of Jesus; so, to attack Israel is to attack the Lamb)*, **and the Lamb shall overcome them** *(speaks of the Second Coming, but also speaks to the fact that Jesus is worthy to administer Judgment and Justice because of what He did at the Cross)*: **for He is Lord of lords, and King of kings** *(proclaims the fact that this 'Lamb' is 'King' of all and 'Lord' of all, and all because of the Cross)*: **and they who are with Him** *are* **called, and chosen, and faithful.** *(Every Saint of God who has ever lived, both Jews and Gentiles, will come back with Christ at the Second Coming.)*

"**And he** *(the Angel)* **said unto me** *(John)*, **The waters which you saw** *(refers back to Verse 1, and presents the word 'waters' being used as a symbolism)*, **where the whore sits** *(if it's not Jesus Christ and Him Crucified [I Cor. 1:23; 2:2], then God refers to it as the 'Great Whore')*, **are peoples, and multitudes, and nations, and tongues.** *(This covers the entirety of the world and tells us that billions have died and gone to Hell as a result of following false religions.)*"

THE TEN NATIONS AND RELIGION

"**And the ten horns which you saw upon the beast** *(pertains to the ten-nation confederation, which will make up the seventh head)*, **these shall hate the whore** *(at least some, if not all, of the ten-nation confederation will come out of the Middle East; Islam rules this part of the world, and it is a rule which has all but destroyed these countries; the implication is the religion of Islam will be put down by this confederacy)*, **and shall make her desolate and naked, and shall eat her flesh, and burn her with fire.** *(This proclaims the fact that the ten nations under the Antichrist will institute and carry out a campaign of elimination as it regards the religion of Islam and, in fact, any other religions in his domain. All of these religions will be replaced by 'beast worship.')*"

THE WILL OF GOD

"**For God has put in their hearts to fulfill His Will** *(while the ten nations have their own agenda, God will use it to bring about His Will)*, **and to agree, and give their kingdom unto the beast** *(the ten leaders of these nations will give their authority to the beast, i.e., 'the Antichrist')*, **until the Words of God shall be fulfilled.** *(This will last 'until' the Great Tribulation has ended, which will be at the Battle of Armageddon in which these nations will be totally destroyed [Dan. 2:34-35].)*

"**And the woman which you saw is that great city** *(refers to rebuilt Babylon portrayed in Revelation, Chapter 18)*, **which reigns over the kings of the Earth.** *(Rebuilt Babylon will not only be one of the commercial centers of the world but, as well, the religious center. The Antichrist will have replaced Islam and other religions with himself as the one being worshiped. It all began at Babylon, and it will all end there [Gen. 11:1-9; Rev. 18:10])*" **(Rev. 17:1-18).**

THE RESURGENCE OF ISLAM

Islam flexing its muscles at this present time is not without tremendous spiritual meaning. As we've already stated in this Volume, it could well be that this religion will greatly help the Antichrist come to power. What the Muslims will not realize is the man of sin has no intentions whatsoever of keeping any promises made to them, but what is one more lie among liars? It must be understood, while the Antichrist will promise many things at the outset of the seven-year Great Tribulation, his promises will mean nothing. He has a goal in mind, and it is to take over the entirety of the world and, as well, to completely annihilate Israel. However, at the same time, he is not going to brook any religion whatsoever, even Islam, because he will set himself up as God and will demand worship.

Concerning this, the Scripture says:

"**Who** *(this is the Antichrist)* **opposes** *(he will oppose every other religion of the world)* **and exalts himself above all** *(above all religions)* **that is called God** *(pertains to his declaration of himself as Deity)*, **or that is worshipped** *(the Antichrist will put down all religions, at least, in the area which he controls, making himself alone the object of worship)*; **so that he as God sits in the Temple of God** *(refers to the Jewish Temple, which will be rebuilt in Jerusalem; the Antichrist will take over the Temple, making it his religious headquarters)*, **showing himself that he is God.** *(This proclaims his announcement of Deity as it regards himself)*" (**II Thess. 2:4**).

HATE THE WHORE

As we stated previously, the Holy Spirit refers to every religion in the world devised by man as *"the great whore."* It must be remembered, it is the Holy Spirit Who chose this designation. The truth is, all religions have been devised by man;

however, Bible Christianity is not a religion, but rather a relationship with a Man, the Man, Christ Jesus. While parts of Christianity have been totally corrupted and are labeled, as well, as *"the whore,"* this applies only to the part of Christianity which looks to other than Christ and the Cross.

John wrote the words, *"And the ten horns which you saw upon the beast, these shall hate the whore."* *"The whore"* refers to the religion of Islam.

We know that some of these ten nations will be in the Middle East and, of course, it is obvious these nations presently are controlled by Islam. However, when the man of sin consolidates his power, which he will with *"the ten horns,"* i.e., *"the ten nations,"* then he will be supreme.

THE TURBULENCE OF ISLAM AT PRESENT

As I dictate these notes on July 29, 2011, the whole world of Islam is in a state of flux. The people in these countries have access to the Internet, and they know what other nations have and know that they do not desire the satanically inspired legalism of Islam. What most of these poor people do not know is that when they overthrow one dictator, they are finding that the Muslim brotherhood is waiting in the wings to take his place. I'm afraid they will find that they have just thrown over one dictator for another. The Muslim world is basically a basket case, politically, economically, and, above all, spiritually. Despite the hundreds of billions of dollars pouring into the Muslim coffers of these oil-rich nations, only a handful of people at the top get the money, with the balance ever going deeper and deeper into poverty. These Muslim leaders are constantly telling these people that the reason they are poverty-stricken is because of America and Israel, etc.

At any rate, when these nations have the upper hand, being controlled by the Antichrist and *"hating the whore,"* which refers in this case to Islam, they will exact their pound of flesh. In other words, there will be no more Islam or any other religion, whatever it might be, in those parts of the world. No doubt, at that time, multiple thousands of Christians will, as well, give their lives for the Cause of Christ. The Antichrist will claim to be God, and untold millions, out of fear for their lives, will claim him as such as well.

NOW IT IS TIME FOR THE FINAL SOLUTION

Now it is time for the Battle to begin. The Antichrist will marshal his forces, which quite possibly will be the greatest army the world has ever known. It will come from the north, the invasion route of countless invaders of centuries past. The Antichrist will be right about one thing, this will be the last invasion, but not like he thinks.

No doubt, the man of sin will have the finest weapons available at that time, with the greatest technological advancements. What Israel will have at that time to defend herself, we aren't told. Presently, she has one of the finest Air Forces in the world, as well as one of the greatest Tank Armies. It is said, as well, that she has approximately 100 atomic bombs, but there is no Scriptural record that atomic bombs will be used in this particular Battle. No doubt, every other type of weaponry will most definitely be used.

THE PROPHECY AGAINST GOG

"Therefore, you son of man, prophesy against Gog, and say, Thus says the Lord GOD; Behold, I am against you, O Gog, the chief prince of Meshech and Tubal *(Ezekiel, Chapter 39, proclaims Gog's defeat by the Lord Jesus Christ. Incidentally, the name 'Gog' is another name for the Antichrist. As well, this is the Battle of Armageddon, even as described in Rev. 16:16)*" (Ezek. 39:1).

As well, *"Meshech and Tubal,"* has no reference to any particular locality, as some have claimed, but, instead, refers to the great confederation of Gentile nations, which have thrown in their lot with the Antichrist in order to destroy Israel.

One of the reasons the phrase is used accordingly is because *"Gog,"* the Antichrist, is a Jew, and, at least, in these circumstances, it is somewhat strange for Gentile armies to follow a Jew, especially, as he attempts to destroy his own people.

Even though there is no particular Scripture that specifically states that the Antichrist will be Jewish, still, it is virtually impossible that the Jews would proclaim as Messiah anyone who is not Jewish, and, at the beginning, they will think this man is the Messiah (Jn. 5:43).

ALL BUT ONE-SIXTH OF THE ARMY OF THE ANTICHRIST WILL BE TOTALLY DESTROYED

"And I will turn you back, and leave but the sixth part of you, and will cause you to come up from the north parts, and will bring you upon the mountains of Israel *(five-sixths of the army of the Antichrist will be killed by the Second Coming of the Lord. 'And will cause you to come up from the north parts,' does not, as previously stated, refer to Russia. It instead refers to the invasion route being the same as it was for the Assyrians, Babylonians, Grecians, and others in the past)*" (Ezek. 39:2).

If it is to be noticed, the Lord emphatically states here through the Prophet Ezekiel, *"I will turn you back."* Later Verses will proclaim as to exactly how the Lord will do this.

While the Antichrist thinks this is his great moment, the moment when he will totally destroy Israel, he is to be in for a rude awakening. In fact, he is being led by the Lord into a trap. To show how much the Lord is orchestrating this event, please notice the Passages:
- *"I will turn you back."*
- *"I will leave but the sixth part of you."*
- *"I will cause you to come up from the north parts."*
- *"I will bring you upon the mountains of Israel."*

All of the time the man of sin will be thinking that he is orchestrating events when, all of the time, the Lord is orchestrating events.

I WILL SMITE YOU . . .

"And I will smite your bow out of your left hand, and will cause your arrows to fall out of your right hand. *(The Antichrist, called 'Gog,' will think he is fighting Israel only, when, in truth, he is fighting the Lord, a battle he cannot hope to win)*" (Ezek. 39:3).

In this Third Verse, the emphasis is on the pronoun *"I."* It is as if the Lord is saying, *"This is enough,"* with Him then unleashing all of His Mighty Power or, at least, enough Power to show the Antichrist and the world just Who the Lord is.

A COMPLETE VICTORY

"You shall fall upon the mountains of Israel, you, and all your bands, and the people that is with you: I will give you unto the ravenous birds of every sort, and to the beasts of the field to be devoured. *(The idea is that the defeat of the Antichrist and his armies will be so severe that vultures and beasts will feed upon the multitudes of dead bodies littering the 'mountains of Israel.'*
"'You shall fall,' signifies not only the defeat of the 'man of sin,' but also the collapse of corrupt human society, which includes corrupt human government)" (Ezek. 39:4).

This will include most, if not all, of the world of that time.
The phrase, *"You shall fall upon the mountains of Israel,"* is a prediction that was given about 2,500 years ago, but, most assuredly, which will come to pass.
Man has ever attempted to rebuild the Garden of Eden but without the *"Tree of Life,"* symbolic of the Lord Jesus

Christ. His efforts have been in vain because it is impossible to do such; however, the grandest effort of all will be in the near future when the Antichrist will make his debut for world dominion. It will be religious, economical, sociological, military, and governmental; hence, at this time, *". . . his number is six hundred three-score and six."* It is *". . . the number of a man,"* denoting man's supreme effort (Rev. 13:18), but it will not succeed as it cannot succeed.

To portray as to exactly how the Lord will fight this battle, let's go back to the previous Chapter, Verse 18.

GOG TO BE DESTROYED AT ARMAGEDDON

"And it shall come to pass at the same time when Gog shall come against the land of Israel, says the Lord GOD, that My Fury shall come up in My Face. *(Once again, this is the Battle of Armageddon. 'My Fury shall come up in My Face,' corresponds to the statement of Zechariah, 'Then shall the LORD go forth, and fight against those nations, as when He fought in the day of battle' [Zech. 14:3])*" (Ezek. 38:18).

This is anger at white-hot pitch, and anger from One Who is all-powerful; therefore, the world is going to see a magnitude of Judgment that it has never known before. The *"man of sin"* will rue the day that he took on *"God's People and God's Land."*

THE FIRE OF MY WRATH

"For in My Jealousy and in the fire of My Wrath have I spoken, Surely in that day there shall be a great shaking in the land of Israel *(the 'great shaking in the land of Israel' can only transpire in the Battle of Armageddon, and only by the Hand of the Lord)*" (Ezek. 38:19).

The phrase of Verse 19, *"For in My Jealousy and in the*

fire of My Wrath have I spoken," is linked to His *"Fury"* and *"Wrath."* These are His People and His Land. He is *"jealous"* over them as He is *"jealous"* over all who belong to Him, including the Church, and we speak of the true Church.

True enough, there will be a great shaking in Israel that, in effect, will be felt all over the world. The entirety of the world at that time will observe all of these happenings by television. We will say more about this momentarily.

"So that the fishes of the sea, and the fowls of the heaven, and the beasts of the field, and all creeping things that creep upon the earth, and all the men who are upon the face of the Earth, shall shake at My Presence, and the mountains shall be thrown down, and the steep places shall fall, and every wall shall fall to the ground. *(This Verse pertains to the Second Coming, which will be the most cataclysmic event in human history)*" (Ezek. 38:20).

The Second Coming will present a display of Power such as the world has never known before.

This tremendous conflict, and we continue to speak of the Second Coming, will affect plant life, animal life, plus all humans, and even the topography of the land. All of this will in no way be caused by the Antichrist, but instead, by the Power of God. Thusly, one can understand the magnitude of *"My Fury that shall come up in My Face."*

Actually, the world has never seen, heard, or known of such Power being expended in such magnitude. No wonder the Lord said, *"The heathen may know Me."* He was referring to much of the world seeing this spectacle over television, more than likely, as it transpires. It will be brought into their very homes all over the world.

TELEVISION

Undoubtedly, there will be hundreds, if not thousands, of

television cameras there, sponsored by the major networks of the world. It will be insisted on by the Antichrist in his pomp and pride as he desires to record, for the entirety of the world, the tremendous victory he is about to win, or so he thinks! However, there will be a Victory, the greatest the world has ever known, but it will not be his!

The tremendous television coverage, meant to impress the entirety of the world, will do just that but in the opposite direction. The world at that time, and we continue to speak of the Second Coming, will see a demonstration of the Power of God as it has never seen before. As well, the world undoubtedly will observe Christ with the Armies of Heaven coming back to Earth in a Glory that boggles the mind.

Actually, outside of these Scriptures, there is no way for one to describe the magnitude of this Power because it is a Power far beyond the capabilities of man to even comprehend or understand.

It may be argued that atomic energy falls into the same category; however, as powerful as that is, it is localized, whereas this will cover the entirety of the land of Israel and, no doubt, many other areas as well!

Some may argue that all the disturbance in the heavens that will take place at the Second Coming, which Jesus addressed in Matthew, Chapter 24, will knock out all television reception. While that certainly could be, there is every evidence, however, that the Lord will protect the television coverage, for the Scripture says, concerning this event, and in the Words of the Lord:

"And then shall appear the sign of the Son of Man in Heaven: and then shall all the tribes of the Earth mourn, and they shall see the Son of Man coming in the clouds of Heaven with Power and great Glory" (Mat. 24:30).

If it is to be noticed, this Passage says, *"All the tribes of the Earth shall mourn, and shall see the Son of Man coming in the clouds of Heaven with Power and great Glory."*

"And I will call for a sword against him throughout all My

Mountains, says the Lord GOD: every man's sword shall be against his brother" (Ezek. 38:21). The evidence here is that during this Battle, the Lord will cause the enemy to begin to fight among themselves.

For instance, when Jonathan was fighting the Philistines, the Scripture says, *"The Earth quaked,"* and, *"they went on beating down one another,"* meaning that the Philistines, for some reason, turned on each other (I Sam. 14:15-16). This will happen, as well, at the Battle of Armageddon.

THE ARTILLERY OF THE LORD

"And I will plead against him with pestilence and with blood; and I will rain upon him, and upon his bands, and upon the many people who are with him, an overflowing rain, and great hailstones, fire, and brimstone. *(This Verse proclaims the fact that the Lord will use the elements, over which neither the Antichrist nor any other man has any control)"* (Ezek. 38:22).

This refers to destructive force of such magnitude that it will cause tremendous bloodshed. In fact, the bloodshed will be so great in the Battle of Armageddon, and we speak of blood being shed by the forces of the Antichrist, that the Scripture says that it will flow to the horse's bridles, at least, for a certain distance. It will, no doubt, be mixed with water (Rev. 14:20).

The terminology of Verse 22 proclaims that which the Prophet Zechariah meant by the Lord doing battle as in the days of old. As He had done so many times in the past, He will do so again at this momentous occasion, as well, and, no doubt, in a far greater way.

For instance, when Sisera, the Canaanite General, was defeated by Debra and Barak, the Scripture says, concerning his 900 chariots of iron, *". . . the Earth trembled, and the heavens dropped, the clouds also dropped water."* It also said, *"The stars in their courses fought against Sisera"* (Judg. 5:4, 20-21).

The Lord will employ the same tactics as these but on a magnified scale. He will use the elements as His Artillery and, to be sure, it will most definitely be effective.

Think about thousands, if not millions, of hailstones falling from the heavens, with many of these stones weighing a hundred pounds or more. Think of the damage they will do. Think about meteorites slashing into the army of the Antichrist and magnify all of that on a scale that's beyond our comprehension. One will then get, at least, somewhat of an idea as to what is going to take place at that time.

THEY SHALL KNOW THAT I AM THE LORD

"Thus will I magnify Myself, and sanctify Myself; and I will be known in the eyes of many nations, and they shall know that I am the LORD. *('Thus will I magnify Myself,' has reference to anger held in check for a long time and then exploding with a fury that defies description)*" (Ezek. 38:23).

The Lord magnifying Himself proclaims this being done by the supernatural destruction of the Antichrist and even all the mighty armies, which are with him. This will be destruction and death never before equaled.

The words, *"magnify Myself,"* and, *"sanctify Myself,"* have terrifying consequences if used in the negative.

We have already alluded to this, but it refers to anger exploding after being held in check for a long period of time. It pertains to the honoring of the Name of the Lord, especially, after the Antichrist has blasphemed him for a period of some seven years.

The phrase, *"I will be known in the eyes of many nations,"* refers to this, which will be done as described, and which, no doubt, and as previously stated, will be portrayed all over the world by television as it is happening.

Therefore, not only will the Antichrist be defeated, but,

due to these actions by the Lord, the entirety of the world will instantly know and recognize His Power, Glory, and Majesty. The Scripture says that He will come back, *"King of kings, and Lord of lords."*

I HAVE SPOKEN IT

"You shall fall upon the open field: for I have spoken it, says the Lord GOD. *('Open field,' refers to the time of the defeat of the Antichrist. It will be in the very midst of the Battle, with the Antichrist bearing down on Jerusalem, thinking that victory is within his grasp.)*

"And I will send a fire on Magog, and among them who dwell carelessly in the isles: and they shall know that I am the LORD. *('Send a fire on Magog,' simply means that the Lord will Personally use the elements of the heavens to destroy the vast Gentile armies following the Antichrist.*

"'And among them who dwell carelessly in the isles,' pertains to other nations of the world, which, in their minds, are neutral and are simply turning a blind eye to this wholesale slaughter against Israel by the Antichrist)" (Ezek. 39:5-6).

THE PROPHET ZECHARIAH

Zechariah, who prophesied about 500 years before Christ, had the following to say as it regarded the Battle of Armageddon:

"Behold, the Day of the LORD comes, and your spoil shall be divided in the midst of you. *('Behold, the Day of the LORD comes,' presents this day as beginning with the Second Coming and lasting until the end of the Millennium. At that time, the end of the Millennium, the 'Day of God' begins and will continue through eternity*

[I Cor. 15:24-28; Eph. 1:10; II Pet. 3:10-13].

*" 'And your spoil shall be divided in the midst of you, '
concerns the Antichrist coming against Israel [Ezek.
38:11-12].)*

**"For I will gather all nations against Jerusalem to
battle; and the city shall be taken, and the houses rifled,
and the women ravished; and half of the city shall go
forth into captivity, and the residue of the people shall
not be cut off from the city.** *(The first phrase refers to the
mobilization of the nations to Armageddon [Ezek., Chpts.
38-39; Joel, Chpt. 3; Rev. 16:13-16; 19:11-21]. 'And the
city shall be taken, ' actually means that the Antichrist will
prepare to take Jerusalem, with actually half of it being
taken. The phrase, 'And the houses rifled, and the women
ravished, ' expresses extreme cruelty practiced by the army
of the Antichrist.*

*" 'And half of the city shall go forth into captivity, '
means that half of Jerusalem will fall to the advances of
the Antichrist, with the other half fighting furiously to save
themselves, but with futility, other than the Coming of the
Lord. Actually, the phrasing of the sentence structure portrays Israel fighting with a ferocity that knows no bounds,
but yet not able to stand against the powerful onslaught of
the combined armies of the man of sin.*

*" 'And the residue of the people shall not be cut off from
the city, ' refers to the army of Israel already cut to pieces
but determined to defend the city, even house to house,
and, if necessary, to die to the last man.)"*

THEN SHALL THE LORD GO FORTH . . .

**"Then shall the LORD go forth, and fight against those
nations, as when He fought in the day of battle.** *('Then' is
the key word!*

● *" 'Then': when Israel will begin to cry to God for
Deliverance, knowing that He is their only hope.*

- " *'Then':* when half of Jerusalem has fallen, and it looks like the other half is about to fall.
- " *'Then':* when it looks like every Jew will be annihilated, with two-thirds already killed.
- " *'Then':* when it looks like the Promises of God made to the Patriarchs and Prophets of old will fall down.
- " *'Then':* when it looks like the Antichrist will win this conflict, which will make Satan the lord of the Earth and, actually, the Universe.

" *'Then shall the LORD go forth,'* refers to the Second Coming, which will be the most cataclysmic event that the world has ever known. *'And fight against those nations,'* pertains to the nations under the banner of the Antichrist, which have set out to destroy Israel, and actually with annihilation in mind.

" *'As when He fought in the day of battle,'* probably refers to the time when the Lord led the Children of Israel out of Egypt by way of the Red Sea [Ex. 14:14; 15:3]. This was Israel's first battle when Jehovah Messiah 'went forth' and fought for them. Israel then passed through a valley between mountains of water; in this, their last battle, they will escape through a valley between mountains of rock, which will be caused by the Second Coming of the Lord)" **(Zech. 14:1-3).**

TELEVISION NETWORKS

We have already alluded to this, but please allow me to elaborate. It is positive that every major television network in the world will be represented at the Battle of Armageddon. The Antichrist, the egomaniac that he will be, will want the entirety of the world to see his great victory as he annihilates Israel. No doubt, he has plans, which have already been formulated, for the greatest gala event the world has ever known, his enthronement as the king of kings and lord of lords. To be sure, it will look like he is going to pull it off.

News reports will come in from the battlefield on a constant basis, with television coverage of his advance going into billions of homes around the world. Steadily, his gigantic army crowds Jerusalem, with news reports going out constantly that victory is near. In fact, half of the city will fall (Zech. 14:2).

It will look like it's all over, and the Antichrist will do what Haman, Herod, and Hitler could not do. It will look like Satan is just about ready to administer the final blow, and these ancient people, Israel, are about to die, and to a man. At that time, the following could very well happen.

There will be a strange phenomenon in the heavens. Jesus Himself said:

"For as the lightning comes out of the east, and shines even unto the west; so shall also the coming of the Son of Man be."

He then said:

"Immediately after the tribulation of those days shall the sun be darkened, and the moon shall not give her light, and the stars shall fall from Heaven, and the powers of the heavens shall be shaken:

"And then shall appear the sign of the Son of Man in Heaven . . ." (Mat. 24:27, 29-30).

IS IT JESUS CHRIST?

The television cameras record the screaming of jets, the powerful explosions of the artillery, and the screams of thousands who are giving their lives as the Jews fight from block to block, from house to house, even from room to room. To be sure, it looks like it is all over for these ancient people. Television is recording it all. The Antichrist wants to make certain that everybody sees his great victory.

And then, thinking that the Antichrist is about to introduce a new type of weapon, thousands of television cameras will, no doubt, point toward the heavens because there, something is happening. Thousands of newscasters will be trying to explain this great phenomenon to all the people of the world, probably stating that this, which the Antichrist is now introducing, will surely mean *"finish"* for Israel.

But then, the terminology will change. It is quite possible that the newscasters and their attempts to explain this phenomenon to the world, even as all of it draws closer, will begin to exclaim, *"Is it possible?"* *"Can it be?"* Then they will possibly say:

"Ladies and gentlemen, see for yourselves. There are millions of white horses, with every one containing a rider, with a startling Glory like we've never seen." But then, they will say, *"There is One leading them, and with a Glory such as has never been witnessed before. And yes, He has a banner stretched around His Body with the name written, 'KING OF KINGS AND LORD OF LORDS!'"*

"Could it be?", hundreds of announcers will say, *"Is it Jesus Christ?"*

And then, the Scripture says:

"Behold, He comes with clouds *(clouds of Saints)*; and every eye shall see Him, and they *also* which pierced Him . . ." (Rev. 1:7).

The phrase, *"Every eye shall see Him,"* could refer to those in Israel and, especially, in the vicinity of Jerusalem. However, due to modern communications, it probably has reference, and, no doubt does, to most of the world, which could only be carried out by television, to which we have alluded.

THE SECOND COMING OF THE LORD

When Jesus came the first time, He came as a lowly human being, raised in the home of peasant parents, which Isaiah prophesied:

". . . And when we shall see Him, there is no beauty that we should desire Him" (Isa. 53:2).

In fact, at the conclusion of His Life and Ministry, He was spit upon, laughed at, caricatured, beaten, ostracized, ridiculed, lampooned, and put on a Cross. However, when He comes back the second time, it will be totally different than the first time. He will then come back in such a Glory as the world has never known before, and as the Scripture has said, *"Crowned King of kings and Lord of lords."* In other words, the Second Coming will be the most cataclysmic event by far that the world has ever known. There has been nothing in history that could even remotely compare with this of which the Bible proclaims.

When it is considered that every Saint of God who has ever lived will come back with Christ, all with glorified bodies, such staggers the imagination.

Millions ask the question, *"Will this really happen?"* The answer is simple.

If He came the first time, and He most definitely did, then for certain, He will come the Second Time (Rev., Chpt. 19).

THE HEATHEN SHALL KNOW THAT I AM THE LORD

"So will I make My Holy Name known in the midst of My People Israel; and I will not let them pollute My Holy Name anymore: and the heathen shall know that I am the LORD, the Holy One in Israel. *(This Verse captures all the Promises made by the Lord to the Patriarchs and Prophets of old!)*" **(Ezek. 39:7).**

There has been no Moving or Operation of the Holy Spirit in Israel or among Jews for nearly 2,000 years. This certainly does not mean that individual Jews have not been Saved because some have come to Christ down through the centuries. However, this was all on an individual basis and had little to do with the great Promises given to the Patriarchs and Prophets of old.

In that coming day, while many things will play a part in all that happens, still, it is the *"Second Coming"* that will open the eyes of Israel and, in fact, the entirety of the world.

The seven years of the Great Tribulation will see the Name of the Lord polluted, blasphemed, and lampooned all over the world as never before. In fact, the Antichrist will actually, in a sense, declare war on the Lord Jesus Christ and do so by slaughtering everyone who names His Name. He will, no doubt, confiscate every Bible where he has any power at all, demanding total allegiance to himself, plus hatred for Christ.

The Scripture says about him:

"And there was given unto him a mouth speaking great things and blasphemies. . . ." It also says, *"And he opened his mouth in blasphemy against God, to blaspheme His Name, and His Tabernacle, and them who dwell in Heaven"* (Rev. 13:5-6).

However, at the Second Coming of the Lord, the *"pollution"* will end once and for all!

THE HEATHEN

The last phrase of Verse 7 says, *"And the heathen shall know that I am the LORD, the Holy One in Israel."* This will proclaim, once and for all, that Jesus Christ is Lord, and everyone will understand that fact.

These very Prophecies in Ezekiel, plus the other Prophets, are little believed by the world. Even much of the church no longer believes that Israel has any part in the great Plan of God; however, this Passage, plus many others, tells us differently!

At the Second Coming of the Lord, to which these Passages refer, so dramatic will be the Lord's Rescue of Israel that the world will have absolutely no doubt as to Who Israel's Saviour is, and neither will Israel!

THIS IS THE DAY WHEREOF I HAVE SPOKEN

"Behold, it is come, and it is done, says the Lord GOD; this is the day whereof I have spoken. *(Verse 8 pertains to the coming Great Tribulation, and more especially to these events at the very conclusion of that particular time, but, more than all, it pertains to the Battle of Armageddon [Zech. 14:7])*" **(Ezek. 39:8).**

Even though these times are yet future, the very near future, and even though these words were uttered some 2,500 years ago, the Holy Spirit would say, *"It is done."*

The events leading up to this time, which, in effect, is the very time in which we are now living, are proclaimed in the Scriptures as being a time of spiritual declension.

Perhaps one could say that economically and numerically, the American church has never been stronger; however, in the spiritual sense, it is at its lowest ebb since the Reformation. Churches are being filled with people clamoring to hear a *"social message."* In fact, the most popular of all is the self-improvement message, as if the old man can be improved. The tragedy is, none of this is the Gospel of Jesus Christ, but rather a Band-Aid that is being placed over the cancer of sin, with the end result being, as always, acute destruction. The real problem with mankind, as it has always been the real problem, is *"sin."* However, the modern church acts as if sin does not exist, with the subject little being broached, except in a nebulous way. All the while, the bondages of darkness are taking their deadly toll, with this Band-Aid of the social gospel not only not helping the people, but rather severely harming them.

THE ONLY ANSWER IS THE CROSS OF CHRIST

As stated, man's problem is sin, whether he is redeemed or otherwise. The only solution for sin, and we mean the only solution, is the Cross of Christ.

Tragedy of tragedies, the Cross is being preached not at all, with some few remote exceptions. Satan does everything within his power to cover up or to sidetrack the true solution. The sad fact is, he, by and large, succeeds with much of the church.

THE SONLIFE BROADCASTING NETWORK

The real reason that THE SONLIFE BROADCASTING NETWORK is being spread all over the world, and at a pace heretofore unheard of, is because of the Message that we preach and teach, THE MESSAGE OF THE CROSS.

If it is to be noticed, the Message that was proclaimed by the Holy Spirit through the Apostle Paul, just before the destruction of Jerusalem by the Roman army, was the Message of the Cross. In fact, this is the Gospel. It's not merely a part of the Gospel or something added to the Gospel. It is, pure and simple, the Gospel of Jesus Christ. In fact, the Apostle Paul defined what the Gospel is by saying:

"Christ sent me not to baptize, but to preach the Gospel: not with wisdom of words, lest the Cross of Christ should be made of none effect" (I Cor. 1:17).

Paul was one of the most educated men to write in the Sacred Text, and yet, when addressing the church at Corinth, he also said:

"For I determined not to know anything among you, save Jesus Christ, and Him Crucified" (I Cor. 2:2).

The reason the Holy Spirit said this through him is simply because the only answer for sin, as stated, is the Cross of Christ, and, please believe me, sin is the problem. The only thing that will set the captive free is the Message of *"Jesus Christ and Him Crucified,"* which must be taken to heart and believed.

Is the modern church preaching the Cross?

No!

We must understand that the Cross brings home the full seriousness of sin, declares the powerlessness of fallen humanity to achieve Salvation, and exposes human delusions of self-righteousness. Nothing else will do that!

In the 1970's, the Pentecostal and Charismatic arms of the Church began to embrace humanistic psychology. In fact, the old-line churches had long since embraced it. We must understand, humanistic psychology is far more than a mere few hours of psychological counseling. It embodies a complete way of life and a complete belief system, all of which is totally opposite of the Word of God. In other words, humanistic psychology is antagonistic toward the Word of God in every capacity. The

Cross of Christ and humanistic psychology cannot coexist. One or the other must go. Tragically and sadly, the Cross of Christ has been thrown aside, in other words, abandoned, in the modern church in favor of humanistic psychology. God help us, especially considering that there is no help whatsoever from that source, only destruction. The Cross of Christ is God's Way, and that Way does not need any help. Humanistic psychology is Satan's way, which is the solution for a world that has forgotten God days without number. It is understandable as to how the unredeemed would embrace such, but not understandable at all as it regards the church.

Peter wrote, *"According as His Divine Power has given unto us all things that pertain unto life and godliness, through the knowledge of Him Who has called us to Glory and Virtue: whereby are given unto us exceeding great and Precious Promises: that by these you might be partakers of the Divine Nature, having escaped the corruption that is in the world through lust"* (II Pet. 1:3-4). Now, either Peter is correct, or Freud is correct. You cannot have both! As Joshua said a long time ago, *"As for me and my house, we will serve the LORD."*

I personally believe that *"the Message of the Cross,"* which we preach and teach, is the Message that the Holy Spirit is presently giving to the church and the world. It's going to be given so powerfully that the church will either have to reject it or accept it. It cannot be ignored! It is the Holy Spirit Who will do that. Let me quote again what the Lord said through the Prophet Ezekiel some 2,500 years ago:

"Behold, it is come, and it is done, says the Lord GOD; this is the day whereof I have spoken" (Ezek. 39:8).

THE AFTERMATH OF THE GREAT VICTORY

"And they who dwell in the cities of Israel shall go forth, and shall set on fire and burn the weapons, both the shields and the bucklers, the bows and the arrows, and the handstaves, and the spears, and they shall burn them with fire seven years *(to think of something being burned 'with fire seven years' allows us to know the extent of the destruction)"* **(Ezek. 39:9).**

Most weapons are made of iron, steel, or other types of metals. Still, there will be enough material that is combustible that it will keep a contingent of people, no doubt appointed for this very task, busy for some seven years.

All of this gives us an idea of how large the army of the Antichrist will actually be, as well as the extent of the destruction that the Lord will bring upon this army.

Even as we have been saying, the Battle of Armageddon will be different than any other battle that has ever been fought. In fact, there has never been anything in history remotely like this, with the exception of when Joshua fought the Amorite Confederation. Concerning that, the Scripture says:

"And the LORD discomfited them before Israel, and slew them with a great slaughter at Gibeon, and chased them along the way that goes up to Beth-horon, and smote them to Azekah, and unto Makkedah.

"And it came to pass, as they fled from before Israel, and were in the going down to Beth-horon, that the LORD cast down great stones from heaven upon them unto Azekah, and they died: they were more which died with hailstones than they whom the Children of Israel slew with the sword.

"Then spoke Joshua to the LORD in the day when the LORD delivered up the Amorites before the Children of Israel, and he *(Joshua)* said in the sight of Israel, Sun, stand you still upon Gibeon; and you, Moon, in the valley of Ajalon.

"And the Sun stood still, and the Moon stayed, until the people had avenged themselves upon their enemies. Is not this written in the Book of Jasher? *(A book no longer in existence, nor any of its copies.)* So the Sun stood still

in the midst of heaven, and hasted not to go down about a whole day. *(It is said that this is confirmed by state documents of Egypt, China, and Mexico, which record this double-day. It is said that Herodotus and Lord Kingsborough, in his history of the Mexicans, and the Chinese philosopher Huai-nan-Tzu quoted these records. The hill of Gibeon, at the moment when Joshua spoke, was behind him to the east, and the sun was setting in front of him to the west. It was evening, and a continuance of the daylight was needed in order to complete the victory.)*

"**And there was no day like that before it or after it** *(through the time of the Bible but not pertaining to this present time),* **that the LORD hearkened unto the voice of a man: for the LORD fought for Israel.** *(God is a Miracle-working God. The Bible opens with Miracles, continues with Miracles, and concludes with Miracles, i.e., 'proclaims them into the eternal future')*" **(Josh. 10:10-14).**

THE SPOILING OF THE ENEMY

"So that they shall take no wood out of the field, and neither cut down any out of the forests; for they shall burn the weapons with fire: and they shall spoil those who spoiled them, and rob those who robbed them, says the Lord GOD" **(Ezek. 39:10).**

In the so-called *"Peace for Galilee"* campaign, when Israel attempted to destroy the PLO, I, along with several of my associates, was invited to Israel where we would be taken into Lebanon at the very height of the conflict. This happened in 1983, if I remember correctly, and was the closest to war that I had ever personally come.

Of all the things seen and experienced, the mile after mile of Israeli tractor-trailers hauling back captured equipment, both damaged and undamaged, was a scene I will not soon forget. Some of the battle tanks looked like they had been opened with a giant can opener, while others seemed to be untouched. As well, there were myriad truckloads of other captured war material, which, no doubt, if usable, was placed in Israel's inventory. At any rate, the amount was staggering, which, at least, gives one an idea as to the fulfillment of this Verse. Whereas the armies just mentioned only numbered tens of thousands, the armies of the Antichrist will number hundreds of thousands, if not millions!

So, if one could multiply what I witnessed those years ago by a thousand, one would have an idea as to what is meant by these predictions. In fact, much, if not most, of the weaponry of the world will be gathered at the Battle of Armageddon.

What is little known by the rest of the world is, at this moment (2011), Saudi Arabia has armed itself, proverbially speaking, to the teeth. In fact, over the last several decades, they have developed several underground bases in their vast land, with the very latest in technological military equipment, and much, if not most, purchased from America. As well, we have just sold Egypt over 100 of the Abrams Battle Tanks, the most sophisticated tanks in the world at this time.

For what does Saudi Arabia and Egypt, for that matter, need such a vast array of the most technologically advanced equipment? She need have no fear from Israel but most probably fears her own fellow Arabs!

The likelihood of a conflict between Arab states, at least, of this magnitude, is unlikely; therefore, the fact that this vast array of weaponry will fall into the hands of the coming Antichrist is a definite possibility. Daniel did say, *"But he shall have power over the treasures of gold and silver . . ."* (Dan. 11:43). All of that, of course, refers to what gold and silver can purchase.

SEVEN MONTHS TO BURY THE DEAD

"And it shall come to pass in that day, that I will give unto Gog a place there of graves in Israel, the valley of the passengers on the east of the sea: and it shall stop the noses of the passengers: and there shall they bury Gog and all his multitude: and they shall call it the Valley of Hamon-gog.

"And seven months shall the House of Israel be burying of

them, that they may cleanse the land.

"Yes, all the people of the land shall bury them; and it shall be to them a renown the day that I shall be glorified, says the Lord GOD" (Ezek. 39:11-13).

No doubt, several millions of men are going to be killed in that which is known as *"the Battle of Armageddon."* Even employing modern equipment to hasten the burial of so many human bodies, still, the stench will *"stop the noses of the passengers."*

Down through the many past centuries, battle after battle has been fought in the land of Israel. The conflict has been almost unceasing for the last 3,500 years, but this will be the last conflict and will, in fact, be the greatest of them all. It will be a conflict totally different than any that has been waged at that particular place or anywhere else, for that matter.

While Israel will definitely be a participant, it will be the Coming of the Lord which will decide this conflict. He will fight in a manner He has not fought since days of old, and will do so in no uncertain terms (Zech. 14:3). Among all the dead, on that great day of Battle, will be *"Gog,"* the Antichrist.

His death will herald the demise of Satan's greatest and final effort to usurp authority over Christ. As well, and at that time, Christ will bind Satan with a *"great chain"* and *"cast him into the bottomless pit, and shut him up, and set a seal upon him, that he should deceive the nations no more, till the thousand years should be fulfilled: and after that he must be loosed a little season"* (Rev. 20:1-3).

GOG

The phrase, *"And they shall call it the Valley of Hamon-gog,"* refers to the Valley of Megiddo, which will be called, at least, for a time, *"the multitude of Gog."* It actually will refer to the multitude slain by God at this great occasion.

The skeptic and unbeliever would have nothing but criticism for the actions of the Lord regarding the deaths of so many in this momentous conflict. However, such will come about only after repeated efforts by the Lord soliciting Repentance, but to no avail! (Rev. 9:20-21)

The destruction of those who have vowed the destruction of God and all that belongs to Him, as well as taking peace from the Earth, thereby, causing the suffering and death of untold hundreds of millions, will be an act of much needed surgery.

Only those who desire unrighteousness and, thereby, further pain and suffering, will take exception to these happenings. At long last, the question, *"How long?"*, will be answered (Rev. 6:10).

As it refers to it taking seven months to bury all the dead, of course, modern equipment could accomplish this task in a few days. However, the latter phrase, *"That they may cleanse the land,"* refers to every bone being found and gathered, which will take *"seven months."*

THE LORD WILL BE GLORIFIED

The phrase of Verse 13, *"And it shall be to them a renown the day that I shall be glorified, says the Lord GOD,"* links this spectacle to the sanctifying of the Name of the Lord.

Normally, the Lord sanctifies His Name by love freely offered and freely received. However, if it is not freely received but, instead, spurned and blasphemously denounced, His Name is *"sanctified"* and *"glorified"* by Judgment.

Therefore, all men will answer to God in one way or the other, whether by Mercy and Grace or by Judgment, but answer, they shall!

THE CLEANSING OF THE LAND

"And they shall sever out men of continual employment, passing through the land to bury with the passengers those who remain upon the face of the Earth, to cleanse it: after the end of seven months shall they search" (Ezek. 39:14).

The executive government of Israel will employ and pay

the men described in this Verse to collect the human bones, wherever found, and bury them in the huge trench or area of Verse 11. This project, as stated, will require seven months.

Also, the phrase of Verse 14, *"Those who remain,"* indicates that at least some of the *"sixth part"* left of the armies of the Antichrist will be employed in this effort of cleansing the land.

THE VALLEY OF HAMON-GOG

"And the passengers who pass through the land, when any sees a man's bone, then shall he set up a sign by it, till the buriers have buried it in the Valley of Hamon-gog" (Ezek. 39:15).

From this Verse, it seems that all the bones will be collected and taken to *"the Valley of Hamon-gog"* and there buried. If this is the case, it will be done for a reason, the portraying of such as a monument of Satan's defeat and the Victory, even the great Victory, of the Lord Jesus Christ.

In fact, this Battle will cover large parts of Israel, with the slain covering many miles, perhaps the entire length and breadth of that country. Quite possibly, it could even spill over into surrounding countries.

"And also the name of the city shall be Hamonah. Thus shall they cleanse the land" (Ezek. 39:16).

The name *"Hamonah"* means *"multitude."* No doubt, it will be a *"city"* of graves, housing the silent dead, and not a city of the living. As stated, it will be a constant reminder of Satan's defeat and the Victory of the Lord Jesus Christ.

A SYMBOLIC GESTURE

"And, you son of man, thus says the Lord GOD; Speak unto every feathered fowl, and to every beast of the field, Assemble yourselves, and come; gather yourselves on every side to My Sacrifice that I do sacrifice for you, even a great sacrifice upon the mountains of Israel, that you may eat flesh, and drink blood.

"You shall eat the flesh of the mighty, and drink the blood

of the princes of the Earth, of rams, of lambs, and of goats, of bullocks, all of them fatlings of Bashan.

"And you shall eat fat till you be full, and drink blood till you be drunken, of My Sacrifice which I have sacrificed for you.

"Thus you shall be filled at My Table with horses and chariots, with mighty men, and with all men of war, says the Lord GOD" (Ezek. 39:17-20).

Verse 17 is the same command as Revelation 19:17-18, 20.

The words, *"the mighty,"* and, *"princes,"* signify the military and political elite of the army of the Antichrist. As well, the *"rams, lambs, goats, and bullocks"* signify the same!

The idea of all of this is, if they would not accept the Sacrifice of Christ at Calvary, then they would be made a sacrifice, which they were. However, it would not save their souls but would serve as a part of the salvation of the world.

Verse 20 refers to the fact that the Antichrist will think to set a *"table,"* portraying the defeat of Israel, but, instead, he and his army will be the *"table,"* i.e., *"My Table,"* i.e., the *"Table of the Lord."*

The idea of all of this is, the powerful confederation of forces gathered by the Antichrist had made plans for the subjugation of the entire world, with certain areas of the world already parceled out to these *"mighty."* These plans have all, and without fail, been foiled by the Coming of Christ. As well, as the Antichrist will be killed, likewise, most, if not all, of his leaders will be killed!

THE SACRIFICE

Four times in Verses 17 through 20, the word, *"sacrifice,"* is used by the Holy Spirit. It is done for purpose and reason.

Christ died as a Sacrifice to save humanity. All who receive that Sacrifice unto themselves and have Faith in its Atoning Offering will be Saved (Jn. 3:16). However, all who refuse to receive it have, in essence, set themselves against God and His Plan for the human family. They will, therefore, be made a sacrifice themselves, as stipulated here, in order that the world rid itself of its malignancy. The sacrifice recorded here in no way saves the victim but, instead, cleanses the world in order that the Righteous may enjoy the Blessings of God.

THE PURPOSE OF GOD

"And I will set My Glory among the heathen, and all the heathen shall see My Judgment that I have executed, and My Hand that I have laid upon them" (Ezek. 39:21).

The Bible regards as *"the heathen"* all who do not accept the Lord Jesus Christ as their Saviour; therefore, that includes almost all of the world.

In effect, every single person in *"Christian America,"* as well as any place else in the world, who does not know the Lord Jesus Christ as their personal Saviour, is regarded by the Lord as *"heathen."* Living in a country, such as America, which adheres, at least, somewhat, to the principle of Christianity, in no way changes the status of the individual person. Only the acceptance of Christ as one's Saviour will change this designation as given by the Holy Spirit.

As well, the idea is put forth in this Passage that the Antichrist has planned to set his glory over the entire world, but, instead, *"Christ will set His Glory among the heathen."*

The phrase, *"And all the heathen shall see My Judgment that I have executed,"* refers to the entirety of the one thousand year Millennial Reign when Christ will rule this world exclusively, and the government shall be upon His Shoulder (Isa. 9:6-7).

However, as previously stated, it, as well, includes most of the world actually *"seeing"* the Second Coming portrayed over television even as it happens.

THE HOUSE OF ISRAEL

"So the House of Israel shall know that I am the LORD their God from that day and forward" (Ezek. 39:22).

Along with *"the heathen"* seeing this glorious spectacle, likewise, *"the House of Israel"* will now *"know"* exactly Who the Messiah is. They will know that the One they rejected and crucified is actually *"the LORD their God."* They will know it *"from that very day and forward."*

As it regards the identification of the Lord Jesus Christ at the Second Coming, there will be no argument. His identity will be obvious, and more specifically, because of the nail-prints in His Hands.

The Scripture says, *"And one shall say unto Him, What are these wounds in Your Hands? Then He shall answer, Those with which I was wounded in the house of My Friends"* (Zech. 13:6).

THE REASON FOR THE TERRIBLE TROUBLES OF ISRAEL

"And the heathen shall know that the House of Israel went into captivity for their iniquity: because they trespassed against Me, therefore hid I My Face from them, and gave them into the hand of their enemies: so fell they all by the sword" (Ezek. 39:23).

With the dispersions under the Assyrians, the Babylonians, and the Romans having been effected by the sword, as well as all who have been exiled through the centuries, and more particularly, the terrible Holocaust of World War II, it can justly be stated, *"They all fell by the sword."*

"They trespassed against Me," refers to Israel's rebellion from the very beginning, which finally necessitated their destruction and dispersion; however, the crowning *"trespass"* of all was their rejection of Christ and His Crucifixion. As a result, they were given over *"into the hand of their enemies,"* where they remained for nearly 2,000 years.

The equity of God's Action with Israel in all periods of their history—past, present, and future—is declared in Verses 23 through 29.

The phrase, *"They trespassed against Me,"* as stated, refers to Israel's rebellion from the very beginning, which finally necessitated their destruction and dispersion. This included the Babylonian captivity, as well as the destruction of Jerusalem by Titus in A.D. 70. However, again, the crowning *"trespass"* of all was their rejection of Christ and His Crucifixion.

Israel refused to believe Christ, and said, *"Let His Blood be upon us, and upon our children"* (Mat. 27:25), and referring to His Kingship, *". . . We have no king but Caesar"* (Jn. 19:15). As a result of them not wanting Him, He *"hid His Face from them."*

In the early 1980's, the Jewish community in the United States grew angry with me because I brought out these very things over our worldwide telecast. They were loath to admit that their terrible problems of the past and present were because of their rejection and Crucifixion of Christ. I answered them as follows.

It is not that the Lord instituted the terrible persecutions that came upon Jewish people down through the centuries, but instead, that they did not desire Him, therefore, He gave them *"into the hands of their enemies."* It was not the Lord Who did these things to them, but their enemies.

They did not want Him, so the only alternative was Caesar, and Caesar has been a hard taskmaster!

"I HID MY FACE FROM THEM"

"According to their uncleanness and according to their transgressions have I done unto them, and hid My Face from them" (Ezek. 39:24).

As they did not desire Him, He *"hid His Face from them."* This was all He could do! Regrettably, this scenario has not yet ended. Continuing to reject Him, Israel will, instead, accept *"another"* as their Messiah (Jn. 5:43). This will happen in the very near future and will bring Israel yet another Holocaust! (Mat. 24:21-22)

However, Israel will finally come out of the darkness into the light and will accept Christ as their Saviour and Messiah. The next Passages tell us how!

It is not that the Lord placed the demonic impulses in the madness of Adolf Hitler that he institute the Holocaust, but that he was the one that Israel chose instead of Christ. They made their decision, and succeeding generations have continued to make the same decision; therefore, as they did not desire Him, He *"hid His Face from them."* This was all He could do! No one can force himself on someone else who does not desire Him. Israel did not desire Him, and they made it very plain as to their wishes; therefore, they, as all others, have reaped the results.

RESTORATION

"Therefore thus says the Lord GOD; Now will I bring again the captivity of Jacob, and have Mercy upon the whole House of Israel, and will be jealous for My Holy Name" (Ezek. 39:25).

He will have *"Mercy"* because of their Repentance, which will take place at the Second Coming. The phrase, *"And will be jealous for My Holy Name,"* is a fiercesome statement. *"His Holy Name"* stands behind His Word. He is *"Jealous"* that His Honor be protected and that every single Prophecy be fulfilled, which they shall!

The word *"now"* of Verse 25 gives us the time that this will happen. It will be after the Battle of Armageddon and at the Second Advent of Christ. This will be the occasion of their humbling before the Lord and His lifting *"the captivity of Jacob."* That *"captivity"* has lasted for about 2,500 years.

Regrettably, none of it had to be but was only because of their *"uncleanness"* and *"transgressions."*

As a result, His Mercy will be so extended that it will include *"the whole House of Israel,"* because *"the whole House"* will repent and accept Him as their Lord and Saviour.

The phrase, *"And will be jealous for My Holy Name,"* as stated, is a fiercesome statement. *"His Holy Name"* stands behind His Word. He is *"jealous"* that His Honor be protected and that every single Prophecy be fulfilled; and, to be sure, that it shall be!

JEALOUSY

The Hebrew root meaning *"jealousy"* portrays a very strong emotion, a passionate desire. The word is used in both a positive and negative sense.

The strong emotion represented by this word can be viewed positively as a high level of commitment when it describes the feelings of a person for something that is rightly his or her own. Here, *"jealousy"* has the sense of intense love. When applied to God, *"jealousy"* communicates the fierce intensity of His Commitment to His People, even when they turned from Him.

In giving the Mosaic Law, the Lord announced to the people of Israel that they must remain committed to Him and not turn to idolatry, and He gave this reason for it:

"I, the LORD your God am a jealous God" (Ex. 20:5). Therefore, the *"jealousy"* of God is expressed in Old Testament history, both in *"punishing"* and in *"showing love."*

CONTINUED RESTORATION

"After that they have borne their shame, and all their trespasses whereby they have trespassed against Me, when they dwelt safely in their land, and none made them afraid" (Ezek. 39:26).

The idea of this and succeeding Verses is the explanation of the word *"now"* in the previous Verse; the *"shame"* resulting from the *"trespasses"* is now over. *"Now"* they can *"dwell safely in their land, and none shall make them afraid."* This will take place in the coming Kingdom Age.

The implication of Verse 26 is that all the *"shame"* was unnecessary and did not need to be. Sadly and regrettably, the Jew has carried this *"shame"* for nearly 2,000 years. They have steadfastly refused to admit that it was because of their *"trespasses."* Consequently, many have been ashamed of their Jewishness or puzzled by the persecutions, thereby, blaming Christ and Christians when, in reality, it's their own *"trespasses,"* which have caused the *"shame."*

Even though the *"trespasses"* are the cause, still, the real cause is the refusal to repent of the trespasses. *"Trespasses,"* sadly and regrettably, are incumbent upon all (Rom. 3:23). It is the lack of the admittance of the *"trespasses,"* and the refusal to come to Christ in order that these *"trespasses"* be handled correctly by Faith in His Atoning Shed Blood, which brings Judgment. Jesus said:

"And you will not come to Me, that you might have Life *(all Life is in Christ; to have that Life, one must accept what Christ has done at the Cross)*" **(Jn. 5:40).**

IN THE SIGHT OF MANY NATIONS

"When I have brought them again from the people, and gathered them out of their enemies' lands, and am sanctified in them in the sight of many nations" (Ezek. 39:27).

This great gathering will take place after the Second Coming of Christ and will include every Jew from every country in the world. They will be brought gladly to Israel. *"And am sanctified in them in the sight of many nations,"* refers to God's Plan for them finally being realized.

In every nation of the world, including America, the Jew is looked at, in many cases, with hostility. This is very wrong but very real!

However, the main reason this phrase, *"Their enemies' lands,"* is used is because the Lord intends for all Jews to be in the land of Israel. That will be totally and completely realized in the coming Kingdom Age.

THEY SHALL KNOW THAT
I AM THE LORD THEIR GOD

"Then shall they know that I am the LORD their God, Who caused them to be led into captivity among the heathen: but I have gathered them unto their own land, and have left none of

them anymore there" (Ezek. 39:28).

So certain is the future Restoration of Israel that the past tense is used in Verse 28 in predicting it.

Verse 28 has reference to Israel finally recognizing Christ as the Messiah and Lord and Saviour. For some 2,000 years, they have steadfastly denied this fact, but, *"Then shall they know."* The word *"then"* signifies the time, as previously stated, as the Second Coming of the Lord.

The phrase, *"And have left none of them anymore there,"* refers to lands other than Israel.

As well, this will not be a forced return but a joyful return, inasmuch as most Jews, if not all, will accept Christ at that time.

THE SPIRIT OF THE LORD

"Neither will I hide My Face anymore from them: for I have poured out My Spirit upon the House of Israel, says the Lord GOD" (Ezek. 39:29).

As previously stated, so certain is the future Restoration of Israel that the past tense is used in Verse 29 in predicting it.

At the Second Coming, indication is, every single Jew on the face of the Earth, the young and old alike, shall come to Israel. All, and without exception, will want to be near their True Messiah. Then they will know Who He is and will have repented of the terrible sin of crucifying Him. The past will be forgotten, and the future will be glorious, but only after the proper Repentance of Israel. In fact, this Repentance is proclaimed in Zechariah, Chapter 12, Verses 11 through 14.

THE POURED OUT SPIRIT

"Neither will I hide My Face anymore from them: for I have poured out My Spirit upon the House of Israel, says the Lord GOD" (Ezek. 39:29).

This Passage and many others emphatically state that Israel will never again go astray because of the *"poured out Spirit of God"* upon them. This Vision opens and closes with a valley of dry bones, which we will address next.

The first Vision saw the resurrection of those bones (Chpt. 37); in the second part of the Vision, nothing but bones will remain, signifying the catastrophic end of the armies of the Antichrist.

So, these two valleys contrast the one with the other—the one, a testimony to God's Faithfulness and Love; the other, to His Fidelity and Judgment.

Verse 29 promises the poured out Spirit of God upon Israel in that coming day. However, it must be understood that the Spirit of God cannot be poured out on anyone until the sin question is first settled. This can only be done by the individual evidencing Faith in Christ and what Christ has done at the Cross. Going God's Way will guarantee the benefits of all His Benefits, which are glorious, to say the least!

CHAPTER NINE

THE RESTORATION OF ISRAEL

If one is to notice, virtually everything about the Battle of Armageddon pertains to Israel. In fact, other than Chapters 1-3, 21, and 22 of the Book of Revelation, it is all about Israel. As it regards Prophecy and the Book of Daniel, that Book, as well, is basically all about Israel. In fact, the Angel said to Daniel, *"Now I am come to make you understand what shall befall your people in the latter days: and yet the Vision is for many days"* (Dan. 10:14).

The reason for all of that is simple. The Lord made Promises to the Patriarchs, the Sages, and the Prophets of old that Israel would see some dark days but that she would be restored. Of course, her darkest days are just ahead, and I speak of the coming Great Tribulation (Mat. 24:21).

In fact, the Holy Spirit through the Apostle Paul dealt with this very thing. He said:

> "For I would not, brethren, that you should be ignorant of this mystery *(what has happened to Israel)*, lest you should be wise in your own conceits *(the Gentiles were not pulled in because of any merit or Righteousness*

on their part but simply because of the Grace of God); **that blindness in part is happened to Israel** *(is the 'mystery' of which Paul speaks)*, **until the fulness of the Gentiles be come in** *(refers to the Church; in fact, the Church Age is even now coming to a close).*

"And so all Israel shall be Saved *(when the Church Age ends and the Second Coming commences; then Israel will accept Christ and be Saved)*: **as it is written** *(Isa. 27:9; 59:20-21)*, **There shall come out of Sion the Deliverer** *(Jesus Christ will be the Deliverer)*, **and shall turn away ungodliness from Jacob** *(Christ will deliver Israel from the Antichrist and, more importantly, will deliver them from their sins)*:

"For this *is* My Covenant unto them *(a Promise)*, **when I shall take away their sins** *(as stated, it will be done at the Second Coming [Zech. 13:1])*" **(Rom. 11:25-27).**

The Thirty-sixth Chapter of Ezekiel portrays the coming Restoration, while this Chapter (Chpt. 37) graphically portrays the spiritual manner of that Restoration.

VISION OF THE VALLEY OF DRY BONES

"The Hand of the LORD was upon me, and carried me out in the Spirit of the LORD, and set me down in the midst of the valley which was full of bones" **(Ezek. 37:1).**

It has been approximately 2,500 years since the Prophet Ezekiel had this Vision and, one might say, it is just now beginning to come to pass but will not be completed until the Second Coming of the Lord. As well, between now and that particular time, Israel is going to face its darkest days yet! However, despite those coming darkened days, which Jesus said would be worse than any had ever been or ever would be, these Prophecies, down to the most minute detail, will be fulfilled **(Mat. 24:21-22).**

Most of Ezekiel's Prophecies begin with the word, *"And,"*

"Also," or *"Moreover."* However, those customary words are missing in this particular Prophecy, indicating something extraordinary, which is obvious.

The phrase in Verse 1, *"In the Spirit of the LORD,"* indicates that this was a Vision and that Ezekiel was not literally taken to this *"valley,"* etc.

The phrase, *"And set me down in the midst of the valley which was full of bones,"* indicates the spiritual and national identity of Israel as being dead.

Even the most rudimentary Bible student would have to recognize the truth of the destiny of these people called *"Jews"* or *"Israelis."* If one knows anything at all about their history, one knows that their survival, other than God, has been an absolute impossibility. Their entire history is one of conflict and persecution, coupled with a sheer determination to remain alive.

Someone has said that the Jew is God's Prophetic Time Clock, and so they are! The only way that these people could have survived through the centuries, and above all, now, as a distinct Nation in their own land is that God has kept them alive for a purpose. That purpose is twofold:

1. To keep the Promises that He made to the Patriarchs and the Prophets (Gen. 12:1-3; II Sam. 7:16).

2. Israel's Restoration will signal the blessings of all the nations of the world under Christ (Ps. 67).

TIMES OF THE GENTILES

When Judah fell to the Babylonian invader, Jehovah took the scepter of power from the hands of the kings of Judah and placed it in the hands of the Gentiles. It has remained there ever since, called by Christ, *"the times of the Gentiles"* (Lk. 21:24).

Upon the Second Coming of the Lord and Israel's acceptance of Christ as Saviour, as Lord, and as Messiah, the *"times of the Gentiles"* will come to a close, with Israel once again assuming the role of world leadership under Christ. This is a position that she need not have lost, save for sin, but will then be restored as this Chapter and so many others proclaim.

The world little knows or understands that the prosperity of all the nations of the world hinges on these people. Consequently, even though they are now spiritually dead and have been for a long, long time, still, God will bless the nation that blesses Israel and curse the nation that curses Israel (Gen. 12:1-3).

VERY DRY

"And caused me to pass by them round about: and, behold, there were very many in the open valley; and, lo, they were very dry" (Ezek. 37:2).

The repetition of *"behold"* fastens the attention upon the two facts:

1. That the bones were very many and very dry.

2. *"Very dry"* speaks of a total absence of Spirituality.

All of this means that what is even now happening to Israel, and what will happen in the near future, is not because of any Spirituality on their part, when, in fact, there is none at all, but rather, signifies that the work is strictly at the behest of the Lord.

Due to them being *"very dry,"* and as a result of having rejected their Messiah, and even crucifying Him, that they have survived the centuries and, especially, becoming a Nation in 1948, is one hundred percent the Hand of God at work.

Even now (2011), there is not an ounce of Spirituality in the land of Israel. In fact, many Jews are atheistic or agnostic.

Even the few who claim to believe the Old Testament are bogged down in legalism and incorrect interpretations of the Bible. Paul said, and we quoted it, *". . . blindness in part has happened to Israel, until the fulness of the Gentiles be come in"* (Rom. 11:25). That blindness is no less now than it was then, if not deeper!

If we are to remember, Paul also said, *". . . all Israel shall be Saved . . ."* (Rom. 11:26). However, we will find that before that comes to pass, Israel is going to see some dark days, actually, the darkest they have ever seen, known, witnesses, or experienced. Jesus said so (Mat. 24:21).

CAN THESE BONES LIVE?

"And He said unto me, Son of man, can these bones live? And I answered, O Lord GOD, You know" (Ezek. 37:3).

Ezekiel's answer to the question of the Lord, *"O Lord GOD, You know,"* signifies that within the realm of human endeavor the task is impossible!

As previously stated in this Volume, an American general viewed the horror of the Nazi death camps in 1945, where some six million Jews were murdered by Hitler and his henchmen. Upon seeing the thousands of dead bodies and the thousands who were near death, he said that this very Passage came to him at that moment, *"Can these bones live?"*

In answer to that question in 1948 and Israel once again becoming a Nation, even after nearly 2,000 years, the Prophecy is beginning to be fulfilled but will not actually be fulfilled until the Second Coming.

Inasmuch as this Prophecy was given shortly after the fall of Judah and Jerusalem, Ezekiel's mind had to have been filled with those recent events. Whether, at that time, he was able to look beyond that moment to a future day so very, very far away, one can only guess. However, once the Vision of the Restoration of the land and the graphic design of the Kingdom Temple was given to him, as is outlined in Chapters 40 through 48, more than likely, his understanding of that future day was greatly increased.

PROPHESY UPON THESE BONES

"Again He said unto me, Prophesy upon these bones, and say unto them, O you dry bones, hear the Word of the LORD" (Ezek. 37:4).

The Prophet is told to *"Prophesy upon these bones,"* meaning that the Lord will give a *"Word,"* which will guarantee their

Restoration and Revival. However, such could only be done according to the *"Word of the LORD."*

As an aside, many have taken this Passage out of context, thinking they could prophesy things into existence according to their own liking, direction, or will; however, such can be only if it is the Will of God. Therefore, the intimation seems to be, if it is God's Will concerning a particular situation, irrespective as to how personal or impersonal it may be, one, according to the Word of the Lord, can prophesy upon the situation, which will hasten its success. However, it is only the *"Word of the LORD"* that has the Power to bring about the miraculous.

When one considers that these words, uttered some 2,500 years ago, are now beginning to be fulfilled before our very eyes, one is made to understand the absolute Power of the Word of God.

YOU SHALL LIVE

"Thus says the Lord GOD unto these bones; Behold, I will cause breath to enter into you, and you shall live" (Ezek. 37:5).

The *"breath"* spoken of is the same breath as when God *". . . breathed into his nostrils the breath of life,"* respecting Adam, and he *"became a living soul"* (Gen. 2:7). The life that is spoken of in this Passage is national life and spiritual life. National life of the Nation has already begun, having its beginning in 1948 and continuing; however, spiritual life will begin in the coming Great Tribulation when 144,000 Jews will accept Christ as their Saviour. The fullness of spiritual life will not come until the Second Coming (Zech. 13:1, 9).

As the Spirit of God is the only One Who can breathe life into unregenerate man who is dead in trespasses and sins, likewise, He is the only One Who can bring Israel back. To be sure, the *"Spirit of God,"* Who moved upon the face of a ruined and formless world (Gen. 1:2), will move upon ruined and formless Israel and, in fact, has already, in a sense, begun to do so!

In his Vision, Ezekiel saw the coming Temple and the River, which will flow out from under the threshold of the Temple, which, in a sense, is a Type of the Holy Spirit. The Scripture continues to say, *". . . everything shall live where the River comes"* (Ezek. 47:1, 9).

As well, to every weary heart, to every thirsty soul, and to everyone who longs for Righteousness, the Lord is saying the same to you that He said of old concerning Israel, *"I will cause breath to enter into you, and you shall live."*

YOU SHALL KNOW THAT I AM THE LORD

"And I will lay sinews upon you, and will bring up flesh upon you, and cover you with skin, and put breath in you, and you shall live; and you shall know that I am the LORD" (Ezek. 37:6).

As stated, this has already begun regarding Israel's national identity but will not begin spiritually until the Great Tribulation, and more specifically, at the Second Coming of Christ.

Actually, this Passage specifically speaks of Israel's national and spiritual identity.

The national identity, which has already begun, speaks of the reconstruction of the external skeleton by bringing together its different parts and clothing them with *"sinews, flesh, and skin."*

However, the second stage, which is the spiritual identity, will not be brought about until the Lord breathes spiritual life into them.

If the first part is already being fulfilled, this means that we are very close to the second stage being fulfilled. If that, in fact, is correct, how close is the Church to the Rapture?

On July 1, 1985, at about 8 o'clock on a Monday morning, the Lord gave me a Vision of the world Harvest and the coming storm. In the Vision, I saw the heavens that were boiling in blackness as I had never seen such before. The Lord told me that He would delay the storm for a short period of time until the Harvest could be gathered.

Even though the Lord did not specifically say such to me, I believe the Vision of the storm, coupled with the *"fields white unto harvest,"* signified the coming Great and Terrible Tribulation.

As we look at these Prophecies, and even the beginning stages of their fulfillment, we know that we're living in the last of the last days.

THE PROPHECY

"So I prophesied as I was commanded: and as I prophesied, there was a noise, and behold a shaking, and the bones came together, bone to his bone" (Ezek. 37:7).

The phrase of Verse 7, *"And as I prophesied, there was a noise,"* actually means *"a voice"* in the Hebrew.

This *"noise,"* i.e., voice, could speak of the *"voice of the Archangel,"* with the *"shaking"* speaking of the Resurrection, signifying the Rapture of the Church.

Actually, Israel will come into full flower at the outset of the Great Tribulation, thinking the Antichrist is the Messiah. This will signify the *"bones coming together,"* even in a greater way. However, as the next Verse suggests, the Antichrist is not the Messiah, and, therefore, he can breathe no breath of life into them but, in fact, will only bring death.

NO BREATH IN THEM

"And when I beheld, lo, the sinews and the flesh came up upon them, and the skin covered them above: but there was no breath in them" (Ezek. 37:8).

The phrase of Verse 8, *"But there was no breath in them,"* concerns their national identity but definitely not their spiritual identity.

In fact, Israel will accept the *"man of sin"* as the Messiah as prophesied by Christ when He said, *"I am come in My Father's Name, and you receive Me not: if another shall come in his own name, him you will receive"* (Jn. 5:43).

The false one whom Israel will receive is the *"another"* spoken of by Christ. As the false Messiah, he can give no *"breath of life."* Only Christ, the True Messiah, can do that!

Actually, as a result of their deception, in the latter half of the Great Tribulation, Israel will come close to annihilation, with the Antichrist turning on them and seeking to destroy them as a people and a Nation.

At that time, according to the Prophet Zechariah, two-thirds will die (Zech. 13:8-9).

"THUS SAYS THE LORD GOD"

"Then said He unto me, Prophesy unto the wind, prophesy, son of man, and say to the wind, Thus says the Lord GOD; Come from the four winds, O breath, and breathe upon these slain, that they may live" (Ezek. 37:9).

"Prophesy unto the wind," actually says in the Hebrew, *"Prophesy unto the Spirit." "Come from the four winds,"* actually says in the Hebrew, *"Come from the four breaths."*

The number *"four"* is symbolic of *"fourfold,"* denoting an absolute, total, and complete Restoration.

The phrase, *"And breathe upon these slain, that they may live,"* denotes the truth that Israel, in the Mind of God, for all practical and spiritual purposes, is *"dead."*

The word *"prophesy"* denotes the *"Word of the LORD,"* which means that it is *"forever settled in Heaven,"* and cannot be denied, and neither can it fail!

Doubt and unbelief would think it absurd, prophesying over *"these bones"*; however, Faith says, *"They shall live."*

"AN EXCEEDING GREAT ARMY"

"So I prophesied as He commanded me, and the breath came into them, and they lived, and stood up upon their feet, an exceeding great army" (Ezek. 37:10).

As the preceding Verses spoke of Israel's national identity, now this Verse speaks of Israel's spiritual identity, signifying their spiritual revival, which will take place at the Second Coming.

The phrase, *"And stood upon their feet,"* speaks of spiritual life enabling such. For a long time, even over 2,000 years, Israel has not *"stood upon their feet"* spiritually, but in that coming Glad Day, they shall! Then they shall be an *"exceeding great army,"* but an *"exceeding great army"* for the Lord.

"THE WHOLE HOUSE OF ISRAEL"

"Then He said unto me, Son of man, these bones are the whole House of Israel: behold, they say, Our bones are dried, and our hope is lost: we are cut off for our parts" (Ezek. 37:11).

"The whole House of Israel," speaks of the entirety of the Thirteen Tribes. The latter part of this Verse, *"behold, they say,"* refers to the latter half of the Great Tribulation. At that time, it will look like the entirety of their Nation will be totally destroyed, with *"hope lost"* and *"cut off for our parts."* This has reference to Zechariah's Prophecy when he said, *"Two parts therein shall be cut off and die"* (Zech. 13:8).

At that time, they will be at the conclusion of the second half of the Great Tribulation. Three and one half years before, they will have suffered a terrible defeat at the hands of the Antichrist, with him taking over Jerusalem and threatening the very existence of these ancient people.

In the Battle of Armageddon, as Ezekiel describes in Chapters 38 and 39, and as Zechariah prophesied, it will look like *"all hope is lost."* Actually, all hope would be lost but for the Coming of the Lord; however, He will come, and, as well, He will have *"healing in His Wings"* (Mal. 4:2-3).

"I WILL OPEN YOUR GRAVES"

"Therefore prophesy and say unto them, Thus says the Lord GOD; Behold, O My People, I will open your graves, and cause you to come up out of your graves, and bring you into the land of Israel" (Ezek. 37:12).

As Prophecy sometimes does, the previous Verse spoke of the last few months or even weeks before the Coming of the

Lord and, therefore, the relief of Israel, whereas Verse 12 goes back even to World War II and forward.

Even though Verse 12 is symbolic of Israel's destitute spiritual condition, it also is literal.

At the end of WWII, with six million Jews slaughtered by Hitler, the Jews became a cohesive Nation some three years later. Then literally began the fulfillment of this Passage, *"And cause you to come up out of your graves, and bring you into the land of Israel."*

Since that time, hundreds of thousands of Jews have come from all over the world, immigrating to the *"land of Israel,"* with the latest excursion from the former Soviet Union not being the least!

As well, the fulfillment of this Passage, concerning the second development, will take place after the Coming of the Lord when every Jew on the face of the Earth will be *"brought to the land of Israel"* (Isa. 11:11-12; 56:8).

AND YOU SHALL KNOW THAT I AM THE LORD

"And you shall know that I am the LORD, when I have opened your graves, O My People, and brought you up out of your graves" (Ezek. 37:13).

"And brought you up out of your graves," has reference in totality to the fact that Israel, for all practical purposes, is all but totally destroyed in the Battle of Armageddon. Actually, there is no earthly way they can be salvaged; however, there is a Heavenly Way! That Heavenly Way is Christ.

This which the Prophet Ezekiel gave to us has never happened in the history of humanity. For some 2,000 years, the Jews were a people who were literally scattered all over the face of the Earth but, still, wherever they were, they maintained their identity. Now the great Prophecies are beginning fulfillment. That within itself is an overwhelming Testimony of the Grace of God, but how many people are listening? How many take any interest in this phenomenon? How many know that it is the Lord's Doings?

The Muslim world is going to find out just Who God really is and, to be sure, they will find out that it's not Allah. As well, they're going to find out that Jesus Christ was and is the Son of the Living God, was and is God manifest in the flesh, and really did die and rose from the dead.

If it is to be noticed, Endtime Prophecies are in many ways different than any other Prophecies. There is a finality about them and a force about them. In other words, all the things against evil that millions have prayed the Lord would do, in that day, that He will do.

MY SPIRIT

"And shall put My Spirit in you, and you shall live, and I shall place you in your own land: then shall you know that I the LORD have spoken it, and performed it, says the LORD" (Ezek. 37:14).

The phrase of Verse 14, *"And shall put My Spirit in you,"* signals the great Revival that will take place in Israel at the Coming of the Lord. The Prophet Zechariah gave in greater detail the happening of this great Moving of the Holy Spirit that's going to come about at that time (Zech. 12:10-14; 13:1, 9).

This will actually be the greatest Revival or Restoration the world has ever known. Almost all Jews, if not all, will accept Christ as their own personal Saviour, thereby, recognizing Him at long last as their Messiah.

The formula, *"says Jehovah,"* is to be understood as a confirmation written at the foot of the Prophecy, saying, *"This is Jehovah's Declaration."*

THE WORD OF THE LORD

"The Word of the LORD came again unto me, saying" (Ezek. 37:15).

The second Prophecy of this Chapter, which, in essence, begins with Verse 15, predicts the future union of the Tribes, their Restoration to the land of Israel, and their settlement there under one Shepherd. It teaches that a Divinely wrought union is real and enduring and brings its subjects into fellowship with God and disposes them around a Divine center, Who and which is Christ.

Of one thing one can be sure, *"the Word of the LORD,"* is that which is going to happen and will do so without fail.

THE TWO STICKS

"Moreover, you son of man, take you one stick, and write upon it, For Judah, and for the Children of Israel his companions: then take another stick, and write upon it, For Joseph, the stick of Ephraim and for all the House of Israel his companions" (Ezek. 37:16).

The *"two sticks"* represent the two Houses of Israel, the northern confederation of Israel, sometimes called Ephraim or Samaria, and the southern kingdom known as Judah. *"His companions,"* refers to Benjamin and Levi, and also possibly Simeon, being joined with Judah. The other Tribes pertain to Ephraim.

The Nation broke apart in about 975 B.C., and did so under Rehoboam, Solomon's son.

Ten Tribes that continued to go under the name of Israel, Ephraim, or Samaria, went their own way (I Ki. 12:16). Jeroboam was the first king of the northern confederation. He was an ungodly man and led Israel into deep idolatry. Actually, the northern confederation didn't have one single godly king.

Judah was left with the Tribe of Benjamin and Levi, the priestly Tribe.

Judah had some godly kings but eventually succumbed to idolatry even as did the northern confederation of Israel.

ONE

"And join them one to another into one stick; and they shall become one in your hand" (Ezek. 37:17).

This Verse predicts that both kingdoms will now become

one kingdom, signifying one people. This can only be brought about by the *"Hand of the Lord,"* which means that they will never again be divided.

As stated, under both David and Solomon, the land was one, but with the death of Solomon, the Nation divided into two kingdoms.

The division remained for about 260 years until the northern kingdom of Israel was taken into captivity by the Assyrians, where it remained, leaving only the southern kingdom of Judah.

Judah lasted for approximately 133 years after Israel's fall before falling to the Babylonians.

After the dispersion of some 70 years, parts of the entirety of the Thirteen Tribes came back into the land and formed one Nation, as they were upon the Birth of Christ.

THE INTERPRETATION

"And when the children of your people shall speak unto you, saying, Will you not show us what you mean by these?" (Ezek. 37:18)

The Holy Spirit through the Prophet Ezekiel is dealing with something that took place nearly 3,000 years ago. Now He will begin to deal with something that hasn't taken place even yet, showing that as far as God is concerned, this is all one story. In the Old Testament, we see Chapter after Chapter devoted to the coming Restoration of Israel. That is why Satan has chosen this avenue, which he thinks is his road to victory. Understanding that there are more predictions and Prophecies, concerning the Restoration of Israel, than anything else in the Bible, he thinks that if he can destroy Israel, this will mean that the Word of God will fall to the ground. If that happens, he has won the conflict.

I realize that many will ask the question, *"But cannot Satan read the Bible, which predicts his total defeat?"* Most definitely he can; however, he simply doesn't believe it. He is self-deceived and has, in reality, deceived most of humanity for all time.

In fact, the Word of God is available basically for the entirety of the world, but most never bother to look at it. If they do, most simply do not believe it. Therefore, they will die eternally lost.

ONE IN MY HAND

"Say unto them, Thus says the Lord GOD; Behold, I will take the stick of Joseph, which is in the hand of Ephraim, and the Tribes of Israel his fellows, and will put them with him, even with the stick of Judah, and make them one stick, and they shall be one in My Hand" (Ezek. 37:19).

The phrase of Verse 19, *"And they shall be one in My Hand,"* proclaims the bringing of these people back together, as the Lord always intended.

The cause was an unlawful breaking off from the House of Judah and the establishment of an independent kingdom. The House of Joseph actually said, *". . . What portion have we in David? and we have none inheritance in the son of Jesse . . ."* (II Chron. 10:16).

At that time, the northern kingdom forsook all that the Covenant stood for, which promised a coming Redeemer, i.e., *"inheritance."*

In effect, they were saying, *"We do not want the Ways of the Lord, we will chart our own course."*

As always, such is the road to disaster. While the Lord dealt with Israel over and over again, in fact, sending to them some of the greatest Prophets who ever lived, still, they continued on their way of idol-worship until they were totally destroyed.

But now, the Lord says that, *"They shall be one in My Hand."*

When God takes groups of His Servants and unites them, they actually become one in His Hand. This means that not only is the old division gone, but the cause of division has also been erased.

"IN YOUR HAND BEFORE THEIR EYES"

"And the sticks whereon you write shall be in your hand

before their eyes" (Ezek. 37:20).

It is amazing that the Lord would take something that simple, such as *"sticks,"* to express and portray something of such vital consequence (I Cor. 1:27).

This will take place at the beginning of the Kingdom Age after Israel has repented before the Lord and knows that their Messiah is, in fact, the Lord Jesus Christ, the very One Whom they crucified.

The Lord would have done this a long time before, but Israel was not ready. After the Battle of Armageddon, when she will come close to annihilation, then, and only then, will she be ready.

It is amazing how that man can rebel against the Lord, bringing upon himself untold suffering and trouble. But yet, we seem to be very slow to learn, if we learn at all.

I WILL GATHER THEM ON EVERY SIDE

"And say unto them, Thus says the Lord GOD; Behold, I will take the Children of Israel from among the heathen, whither they be gone, and will gather them on every side, and bring them into their own land" (Ezek. 37:21).

The total fulfillment of this will take place in the coming Kingdom Age.

Despite the Nation of Israel being formed in 1948 and millions migrating during this period of time to that land, still, there are other millions of Jews scattered all over the world. Many of these Jews have little regard for the Lord or His Word. However, at the beginning of the coming Kingdom Age, with Jesus Christ having come back to this Earth with such Splendor and Glory as to defy all description, a spiritual awareness will then be born in the hearts of every Jew on the face of the Earth. As we have said previously, if the truth be known, more than likely, most Jews presently are atheistic or, at least, agnostic. That will all change with the Second Coming. In fact, the rebirth of Israel, and one might say the rebirth of the Jews, will be possibly the greatest Revival the world has ever known in all of its history. There is evidence that every Jew on the face of the Earth, and to a man, will accept Christ as Saviour, as Lord, and as Messiah. At the same time, they will strongly desire to go to Israel to form the new Nation under Christ, and I may quickly add, also under David, which we will see. In fact, at that time, Israel will be the greatest Nation in the world, actually, the priestly Nation of all of mankind.

When Israel is in her rightful place, *"Then shall the Earth yield her increase; and God, even our own God, shall bless us"* (Ps. 67:6).

A most remarkable Revelation is given to us in this Passage in Psalms. Much of the world presently is plagued by drought, famine, and starvation.

With Israel in her proper place and the kingdoms of this world praising the Lord, then the *"Earth will yield her increase,"* and there will be abundance for all!

ONE NATION

"And I will make them one Nation in the land upon the mountains of Israel; and one King shall be King to them all: and they shall be no more two Nations, neither shall they be divided into two kingdoms anymore at all" (Ezek. 37:22).

"In the land," refers to the land of Israel, as promised to Abraham (Gen. 12:7).

What exactly did the Lord promise to Abraham? He promised the following:

The boundary on the west, as would be obvious, is the Mediterranean; on the south, the Suez Canal, which includes the Arabian Peninsula; on the east, the Euphrates River, which takes in a great part of modern Iraq plus Jordan; on the north, the northern border of Lebanon plus Syria.

As is obvious, that promised to Abraham is a great deal larger than the present area referred to as Israel. Actually, it is probably about 100 times larger.

David came closer to occupying the entirety of the Promised

Land than anyone else! However, for the greater part of its existence, the territory was much reduced, incorporating basically what was called *"from Dan to Beer-sheba."* In the coming Kingdom Age, all of the original promised territory will be occupied, with possibly even extra space added. As well, the Arabian Peninsula, which now is all desert, but which is approximately 60 to 70 times larger than present-day Israel, will then blossom as the rose (Isa. 35:1). In other words, the Lord will turn this desert, plus all other deserts of the world, into a verdant garden.

Due to this being promised by the Lord to the sons of Jacob, Satan has contested it mightily! Of course, the entirety of the world is aware of the territorial demands made by the Muslims in Israel and their being granted the Gaza Strip plus Jericho, with the entirety of the West Bank claimed as well.

It is ironic that in July, 1994, the newly formed State of Palestine advertised the City of Jerusalem as Jerusalem, Palestine. Israel was highly offended by this action, as it should have been! However, it is well-known that the nations of the world will not recognize Jerusalem as the capital of Israel, instead looking to Tel Aviv.

Irrespective of the present claims, this land belongs to Israel and is promised by the Lord, which Promise, to be sure, will be carried out and fulfilled in totality (Gen. 12:7).

Of course, this is where the contention begins. The Muslims claim that Ishmael is the promised seed, and they are due the land, while Israel claims, according to the Bible, that Isaac is the promised seed, therefore, the land belongs to them. To be frank, this problem will not be settled until the Second Coming and, to be sure, it will at that time be settled.

Incidentally, the Arabs in Israel refer to themselves as *"Palestinians,"* but the truth is, there are no such people by that name. The people who occupy part of Israel, calling themselves *"Palestinians,"* are in actuality Jordanians, Egyptians, Syrians, etc.

The following is an article written by John Rosenstern, an Associate Minister of Jimmy Swaggart Ministries, and published in the July, 2011, issue of *"The Evangelist,"* the monthly publication of this Ministry. It is as follows, and I think will shed some light on this thorny question as to who owns the land called *"Israel."*

THE LAND IS MINE

"The Middle East has been a festering powder keg for centuries. Now, more than ever, it seems ripe for an all-out confrontation between Israel and her surrounding Muslim neighbors. The land comprised of Modern Israel, Palestine, Jordan, Syria, Lebanon, Iraq, Arabia, and small parts of other neighboring countries was promised by God, in the Bible, to Israel. Events in the last 100 years have shaped the modern real estate of the Middle East; however, there's one small parcel of the land in the Middle East that is still in dispute, Israel. What legitimate claim do the Jews have to their land? Do the Palestinian people truly have a history in this land, and therefore, a right of succession? How does God figure into this equation? I hope to address these questions, and many others, as we explore from the Bible what God has to say about the land ownership and whose right it is to claim the land. I believe a careful evaluation of this matter will expose the root of the problem that existed from the time of Abraham unto this day.

GOD'S LAND

"'The Land is Mine' was a declaration by God to Israel, and to us all, that there is a legitimate land owner. Throughout the Bible, God establishes who owns the land, to whom the land is promised, and the conditions that must be obeyed to remain in possession of the land known as Israel (Jer. 7:7; 11:5; Hos. 9:3; Joel 1:6; 2:18; 3:2; Ezek. 38:16). History has proven that the land has been possessed or controlled by many different nations at many different times. Right now the land is possessed by Israelis and Palestinians; however, the influence from the surrounding

nations of Syria, Egypt, Lebanon, Saudi Arabia, Iran; and the United States, England, Russia, and many other nations, including the United Nations, have played a crucial role towards resolving who they think should possess the land.

IF THE JEWS RETURN

"Modern Israel was formed on May 14, 1948, in postulation of the United Nation's decision to partition the land between Israel and the Palestinian people. A two state solution was determined as the peaceful resolution for the disputed land. The Palestinians rejected Israel's right to be a Nation and protested by refusing to form a nation themselves. Israel declared her independence and the birth of modern Israel took her first traumatic breath with a struggle to survive, not just as a Nation but as a people. The Confederate Muslim armies of the newly shaped Middle East immediately sought to destroy Israel and prevent her from becoming a Nation. Efforts by Nazi Germany during WWII failed to abort the Jews while they were in the womb of hope of being a Nation. Adolf Hitler, while accompanied by his Muslim companions, Haj Amin Al Husseini and Hasan Al Banna, formulated a 'Final Solution' to exterminate Jews from the Planet. Although nearly 6,000,000 Jews died during Hitler's reign of terror, Jews drew strength from their survival as a people, and hopes of being a Nation once again finally became reality.

OCCUPATION TERMS

"The Land is Mine will consider God's Covenant Promises to Abraham, Isaac, and Jacob. These Patriarchs of old were given immutable Promises that their seed would have 'lease' rights to God's land forever. The conditions were clearly spelled out by God and the terms were not to be broken lest the tenant suffer temporary eviction. Each dispensation of the generations that succeeded Abraham were given responsibilities to satisfy the land lease terms so to speak. Dwelling in the land with obedience had

many privileges and benefits. Unlike today where an apartment renter may get Cable TV and electric power thrown in as part of the lease package, Israel was promised financial prosperity, good health, and peace among itself and its enemies. In fact, the whole world was promised these benefits as long as Israel remained obedient to the lease terms and remained in the land (Ps. 85:1-13).

NO PEACE

"Today Jews dwell in the land promised by God to her fore-fathers; yet she is without peace. The world speaks of peace at every forum and conclave; yet it is without peace. What is peace and what constitutes peace will be addressed throughout The Land is Mine. To illustrate how true and lasting peace can be achieved and maintained by individuals, and the nations of the world, history must be noted.

"History has demonstrated that under the leadership of dictators, monarchs, and governments there have been times of peace. However, during those times, financial prosperity, personal health, and freedom were not obtained by everyone. Even while under Pax Romana the Roman Empire sustained a façade of peace. Rome's egregious emperors ruled in dictatorial fashion by subduing surrounding countries and demoralizing the general public at will; while heralding this as peace (?) for us to laudably claim peace on Earth and goodwill toward man, while using corrupt governments as our guide, is as foolish as putting a compass in your car while you plan to drive your car to the moon.

ISRAEL'S RIGHT IN THE LAND

"There are many claims to the land of Israel. Muslims claim Jerusalem houses their third holiest site. The world recognizes Jerusalem as an international city. The Bible declares Jerusalem will be a 'burdensome stone for all people.' Middle East peace has plagued every President since the founding of the United

States of America. The expansion of the US Navy after the Revolutionary War was to free our seafaring mercantilists from the Muslim pirates of the Barbaric Coasts.

"The name of Israel is mentioned over 1600 times throughout the Bible while Jerusalem is mentioned over 800 times. The city of Jerusalem is called 'The City of David' over 40 times. There should be little argument to the significance of Israel and Jerusalem for God's sake, according to the Bible.

"God's immutable Promise to Abraham, Isaac, Jacob and his children, and David will not be broken or substituted by the Christian Church. God has a Plan to bring Israel to its rightful and legal possession of the land. The day is coming soon when Israel will reign in God's Righteousness and possess God's Land in peace. Only then will there be world peace (Deut. 30:1-6; Isa. 11:11-16).

ABRAHAM

"There are three faiths in the world that trace their origins to Abraham. Jews, Christians and Muslims all claim father Abraham to be significant to the establishment of their beliefs. Jews and Christians obtained the majority of their knowledge about Abraham from the Old Testament of the Bible, also called the Tanakh in Hebrew. Muslims hold to the Koran as their sacred book. Muslims believe their prophet Mohammed received revelations from Allah, his god, and memorized Allah's instruction and then dictated the sayings to others. Later these revelations were compiled into a book after Mohammed's death and called the Koran. Muslims believe Jews and Christians have twisted and perverted the original meaning of the Bible; therefore, Allah sent down the Koran to bring back the proper understanding of his will for man. In Islam Mohammed is revered above all prophets and is considered to be the last and greatest of all prophets. Muslims also revere Abraham as a Prophet and a version of his life is found throughout the Koran. Abraham's name occurs 69 times in the Koran making him the second most occurring name of Prophets in the Koran after Moses. There are many fundamental

differences between the Bible story of Abraham and the Muslim story in the Koran. Both accounts contradict each other. They are mutually incompatible.

THE KORAN

"The Koran is written in Suras, similar to Chapters. The verses of the Koran are called Ayats. There are 114 Suras in the Koran. The structure of the chapters is not in historiological or chronological order. The Suras, with the exception of the first one, are arranged by length. Chapter 2 is the longest, on down to the last Sura. Due to the lack of chronology the Koran is not designed to be a story. The very name Koran means to recite. It is more a book of commands than a story line of historical events. The Hadiths, sayings and traditions of Mohammed, were assembled by followers of Mohammed after his death. The Hadiths provide some historical perspective that transpired throughout Mohammed's life. The Hadiths explain the historical events in the Koran.

ABRAHAM AND ISAAC

"In Sura 6:74 the Koran claims Abraham's father's name was Azar and not Terah as in the Bible, Genesis 11:24, 31. Sura 14:37 says Abraham worshipped in the valley of Mecca. Mecca is located in modern day Saudi Arabia. A distance of over 750 miles separates Mecca from Israel. There is no historical evidence whatsoever that Abraham ever was in Mecca.

"The Bible clearly says in Genesis 13:18, Abraham worshipped Jehovah God in Hebron. The well-known story of how Abraham was commanded by God to offer Isaac as a sacrifice is detailed throughout Chapter 22 of Genesis. Jehovah God made it very clear that Abraham was to take his 'only son Isaac' into the land of Moriah and offer him there for a burnt offering. Isaac was God's Child of Promise. It was to be through his lineage that God's Promise to Abraham would be manifest. The

contravening testimony of the Koran teaches in Sura 37:100-112, that Abraham offered Ishmael and not Isaac as a sacrifice.

DISCREPANCIES

"Two more important discrepancies that distinguish the Bible from the Koran are not found in the Bible. In fact they are ambiguous and historically incorrect. The Koran claims Abraham built the Kabah, Sura 2:125-127. The Kabah was located in Mecca and was a shrine where 360 gods were worshipped among the Arab Bedouins. Mohammed's family were the caretakers of the Kabah, according to Islamic tradition. One of the gods of the Kabah was Allah. Mohammed's father was named after Allah. It is not mentioned anywhere in the Bible. The only remote similarity in the stories of Abraham and Isaac in the Bible and Koran are simply their names.

"The other story of Abraham's life taken from the Koran is a claim that he was thrown into a furnace by Nimrod, Sura 21:68-69 and 9:69. This fairy tale is not found in the Bible but is plagiarized by Mohammed from Jewish tradition. This story is found in the Midrash Rabbah.

PROMISES

"The Bible gives a lengthy story of Abraham and the Promises of God to him and his seed. The calling of Abraham came to him while he was a Gentile living in Ur of the Chaldees. Ur of the Chaldees was located in modern day Iraq not far from Babylon. God instructed Abraham to leave his family and go to a land that God would show him. The Promise of God to Abraham begins with a destination, Canaan Land, known today as modern Israel or Palestine. We can immediately observe from the call to Abraham that it is linked to a Promised Land. The Promises given by God of Abraham required his obedience to God. If Abraham leaves his family and father's house, and travels to the land God would show him, he would become a great nation and

his name would be blessed, and he would be a blessing to the world. God would add to the Promise given to Abraham with a special Blessing to those who would bless Abraham. Likewise, God would curse those who curses Abraham (Gen. 12:1-3).

THE ALTAR

"Abraham was to leave the worship of idols and separate himself from his family unto God. In order to better comprehend the deep meaning associated with Abraham's relationship to God we must first understand how Abraham worshipped God through Sacrifices. The first evidence we have of Abraham sacrificing to God is when Abraham passed through the land of Canaan. God appeared to Abraham and strengthened His Promise to him by telling him his seed, children, and future posterity, would also inherit the land. Abraham built an altar unto God. The Hebrew for Altar means a place of slaughter, signifying a place used for Sacrifices. The Sacrifice was a memorial to God for His deeds toward Abraham. The Sacrifice denotes Abraham recognized God as God. His relationship was based on trust and obedience to God. The Patriarch knew God and honored Him with worship through Sacrifices. It is essential for us to realize that throughout Abraham's life the wonderful loving fellowship he shared with God was never without his Sacrifices to God.

THE SACRIFICE

"What did God supply to Abraham as an assurance that he would inherit the land? Faithful Abraham asked God, 'whereby shall I know that I shall inherit it?' God would take him to the Sacrifice. I say the Sacrifice because the Promise God would make to Abraham would only be assured by the Cross. The Cross is the 'only' means that we can receive anything from God. The very word Covenant means 'a cut' indicating Sacrifice. God instructs Abraham to take certain animals and to cut them in half and lay them apart. God would then cause a deep sleep to fall upon

Abraham and God would tell Abraham the things that would happen to his seed and the delay for them to inherit the land.

THE WORD OF GOD

"*Genesis 15:13-21* – 'And He *(the Lord)* said unto Abram, Know of a surety that your seed shall be a stranger in a land that is not theirs, and shall serve them; and they shall afflict them four hundred years *(the four hundred years pertained to the time from the weaning of Isaac to the deliverance of the Children of Israel from Egyptian bondage; the time frame covered the time spent both in Canaan, before it belonged to them, and Egypt, as well)*;
"'And also that nation, whom they shall serve, will I judge *(Egypt)*: and afterward shall they come out with great substance *(much gold and silver would be given to them by the Egyptians when they left [Ex. 11:1-3])*' (**Gen. 15:13-14**).

"God, in His Infinite Mercy, would forestall His Judgments among the nations that possessed the Land He promised to Abraham. God's Mercy is patient and He is longsuffering not willing that any should perish, but that all should come to repentance. In His foreknowledge, God knew that the Amorites would not repent, but He still gave them many years of opportunity.

A MODERN DILEMMA

"Is it any different presently? The world court of public opinion holds Israel as interlopers, illegal occupants, and oppressors in the land God promised them. The world is vastly moving towards isolating Israel by forcing her to part her land to a people who have no history. The so-called modern Palestinian people have no historical language of their own. They have no currency as well to call their own. They are not mentioned as a unique people in even one history book. For example, on March 31st, 1977, the Dutch Newspaper 'Trouw' published an interview with Palestine Liberation Organization executive committee member,

Zahir Muhsein. Here's what he said.

"'The Palestinian people do not exist. The creation of a Palestinian state is only a means for continuing our struggle against the state of Israel for our Arab unity. In reality today there is no difference between Jordanians, Palestinians, Syrians and Lebanese. Only for political and tactical reasons do we speak today about the existence of a Palestinian people, since Arab national interests demand that we posit the existence of a distinct "Palestinian people" to oppose Zionism.

"'For tactical reasons, Jordan, which is a sovereign state with defined borders, cannot raise claims to Haifa and Jaffa, while as a Palestinian, I can undoubtedly demand Haifa, Jaffa, Beer-sheba and Jerusalem; however, the moment we reclaim our right to all of Palestine, we will not wait even a minute to unite Palestine and Jordan.'

THE COVENANT

"In the meantime the custom of the Covenant (B'rith) was understood to be two parties entering into an agreement and sealing the agreement through a sacrifice. The animals were cut in half with their blood spilling out on the ground. The pieces of the severed animal bodies were then laid apart on either side of the blood soaked ground. The parties in covenant then walked between the sacrificed animals on the blood; signifying that if one breaks the oath the same judgment that the animals experienced would happen to them. The most fascinating aspect of God's Covenant to Abraham was that God walked through the animals while Abraham was asleep, '. . . behold a smoking furnace, and a burning lamp that passed between those pieces.' The burning lamp represented the Judgment of God. God then makes another Covenant with Abraham that promises the land will also go to Abraham's seed for an inheritance.

COVENANT BORDERS

"There is, no doubt, from God's Word that God set the borders

(Gevulot Ha-aretz) of the land He promised to Abraham and his seed, '. . . from the river of Egypt unto the great river, the River Euphrates.' The Bible gives account of the borders in several places: Genesis 15:18-21; Exodus 23:31; Numbers 34:1-15; and, Ezekiel 47:13-20, to name a few. For us to better appreciate the vast geography involved with the land inheritance we must look at the boundaries a little closer.

"Early Jewish tradition, expressed in the commentaries of Russia and Yehuda Halevi, coupled with the Aramaic Targums (Jewish Commentaries), understood the 'Brook of Egypt' (Nachal Mitzrayim), as mentioned in Numbers, Deuteronomy, and Ezekiel as the Nile River in Egypt. Based on this information the expanse of the land promised to Abraham extended from the Nile River in Egypt to the Euphrates River in Iraq. God would further mention to Abraham the nations of peoples that then possessed the land, 'The Kenites, and the Kennizzites, and the Kadmonites, and Hittites, and the Perizzites, and the Rephaims, and the Amorites, and the Canaanites, and the Gergashites, and the Jebusites.' In modern geographical terms Abraham and his seed would inherit part of Egypt (the Sinai), Israel, Palestine, Jordan, Lebanon, Syria, and a large portion of Iraq, up to the River Euphrates, which also includes the Arab Peninsula.

MODERN BORDERS

"Prior to World War I all of these nations were part of the Islamic Ottoman Empire. After the war the land mass was taken from the Ottoman's who threw their lot in with Germany and the axis, and then divided between France and England in what was known as the Sykes-Picot agreement.

"*It was agreed that France was to exercise direct control over Cilicia, the coastal strip of Syria, Lebanon, and the greater part of Galilee, up to the line stretching from north of Acre to the northwest corner of Lake Kinneret (Sea of Galilee), referred to as the 'blue zone.' East of that zone, in the Syrian hinterland, an Arab state was to be created under French protection (Area 'A').

Britain was to exercise control over southern Mesopotamia (the 'red zone'), the territory around the Acre-Haifa bay in the Mediterranean, with rights to build a railway from there to Baghdad. The territory east of the Jordan River and the Negev, south of the line stretching from Gaza to the Dead Sea, was allocated to an Arab state under British protection (Area 'B'). South of France's 'blue zone,' in the area covering the Sanjak of Jerusalem, and extending southwards toward the line running approximately from Gaza to the Dead Sea, was to be a 'brown zone' under international administration. (*Jewish Virtual Library)

CHRIST OUR COVENANT

"The unique Covenant God made was not so much 'with' Abraham and his seed but 'to' Abraham and his seed. Abraham did not walk through the sacrificed animals. God alone swore unto Himself that He would give an inheritance to Abraham. Throughout the history of the Bible God would repeat Himself through various writers that He would remember His Covenant with Abraham and, thereby, extend Mercy to his seed.

"Jesus Christ in the New Covenant, would likewise fulfill a unique Covenant by representing both God and man, in the New Covenant (II Cor. 5:19)."[1]

In actuality, all of this points to the Lord Jesus Christ; however, and as is obvious, the Muslim world does not recognize Jesus Christ as the Son of God. But, if it all boils down to the bottom line, so to speak, eventually and ultimately it all centers up on the Lord Jesus Christ. His coming back will decide this problem.

THEY SHALL BE MY PEOPLE, AND I WILL BE THEIR GOD

"Neither shall they defile themselves anymore with their idols, nor with their detestable things, nor with any of their transgressions: but I will save them out of all their dwellingplaces, wherein they have sinned, and will cleanse them: so shall they

be My People, and I will be their God" (Ezek. 37:23).

When Christ comes back to this Earth, which He most definitely will, as we have stated, Israel will accept Him as Saviour, Lord, and Messiah. At that time, the Lord *"will cleanse them."* The great Prophet Zechariah gives us more insight into this. He said:

"In that day there shall be a Fountain opened to the House of David and to the inhabitants of Jerusalem for sin and for uncleanness" (Zech. 13:1).

"In that day," occurs 18 times from Zechariah 9:16 through 14:21. This shows how precious *"that day"* is to the Messiah's Heart. In that day, His Victory over the enemies of His People will be great, but greater will be His Moral Victory over His People themselves.

The Christian's true triumphs are God's Triumphs over him, and God's Triumphs over His People are our only victories. Such was Jacob of old, who represented Israel in that coming Glad Day. The Conversion of the Apostle Paul illustrates the future Conversion of Israel. He hated Jesus, but on the Damascus Road he looked upon Him Whom he had pierced; and he mourned and wept.

THE OPENED FOUNTAIN

The phrase, *"In that day there shall be a Fountain opened,"* does not mean that it is first opened there, but that Israel will only begin to partake of it *"in that day,"* i.e., the beginning of the Kingdom Age. This Fountain was historically opened at Calvary but will be consciously opened to repentant Jews in the future day of her Repentance, for the fact and function of that Fountain only becomes conscious to the awakened sinner.

THE NEED FOR CLEANSING

A true sense of sin and guilt in relationship to God awakens the sense of the need of cleansing, and so, the shed and cleansing

Blood of the Lamb of God becomes precious to convicted conscience. As well, the ever-living efficacy of Christ's Atoning Work, with its Power to cleanse the conscience and the life, is justly comparable to a fountain and not to a baptismal font. The sense of the Hebrew Text is that this Fountain shall be opened and shall remain open.

ALL MAY COME

"To the House of David and to the inhabitants of Jerusalem for sin and for uncleanness," portrays the possibility that, of all sinners, the Jerusalem sinners may be accounted the greatest. It was Jerusalem that stoned the Prophets and crucified the Messiah; therefore, great sinners may hope for pardon and cleansing in this Fountain opened for the House of David.

The entrance of Christ judges sin, unmasks its true character, and arouses a moral consciousness which approves that Judgment. That entrance dominates, adjusts, disciplines, instructs, and cleanses man's affections, relationships, and desires. All of this must be cleansed, not only in Israel of a future day, but also in any and all who come to Christ. That Fountain is open to all!

DAVID

"And David My Servant shall be king over them; and they all shall have One Shepherd: they shall also walk in My Judgments, and observe My Statutes, and do them" (Ezek. 37:24).

"And David My Servant shall be king over them," is meant to be taken literally. David was ever looked at as the example for all the kings of Israel and, consequently, will serve in this capacity under Christ forever.

A self-righteous church would have difficulty understanding this, especially due to David's transgression regarding Bath-sheba and her husband Uriah; however, only self-righteousness would blanch at such a prospect. To those who truly understand who and what man actually is and that the Grace of

God is our only Hope, this Passage is a source of great comfort.

Even though David suffered terribly so for this transgression, still, this sin, plus all the other sins that David committed, were washed away by the Precious Blood of Jesus Christ. It is called, *"Justification by Faith,"* and is the undergirding strength of all who trust in the Name of Christ.

JUSTIFICATION BY FAITH

The great question is, *"How can God, Who must ever abide by His Righteous Nature, declare a person who is obviously guilty as 'not guilty'?"*

Paul said, *"To declare, I say, at this time His Righteousness: that He might be just, and the Justifier of him who believes in Jesus"* (Rom. 3:26).

So, the same question may be asked in this way, *"How can God be just and, at the same time, be the Justifier of the person who is obviously guilty?"*

The answer is found in the latter portion of Romans, Chapter 3, Verse 26, *"who believes in Jesus."*

Justification is a declaration of *"not guilty,"* and to take it even further, it actually means, *"Totally innocent, having never been guilty of any transgression or iniquity."*

Now we ask the question again, *"How can God maintain His 'Justice' and, at the same time, justify guilty sinners?"* Once again, the answer is found in Christ and Christ Alone. More particularly, it is found in what Christ did at the Cross.

SUBSTITUTION AND IDENTIFICATION

For this great work to be carried out, the Work of Justification, God would have to become Man, which we refer to as *"the Incarnation."* He would have to be man's Substitute, doing for man what man could not do for himself. For proper Justification to be carried out, Christ would have to be born of a Virgin, exactly as prophesied by Isaiah (Isa. 7:14). Her name was Mary! His birth had to be in this manner in order that He not have original sin, which came upon all men after the Fall. It is referred to as the *"fallen sons of Adam's lost race."*

As the Perfect Son of God, in fact, the *"Last Adam,"* Jesus had to keep the Law perfectly and in every respect. In other words, He could not sin in word, thought, or deed. Had He done so, not only would man be eternally lost, with no possible way for anyone to be Saved, but, likewise, God would be defeated, with Satan becoming the Lord of the Universe. So, everything was riding, so to speak, on the Lord Jesus Christ. In other words, God placed everything in Jesus Christ and did so because of His Great Love for fallen humanity (Jn. 3:16).

Not only did Christ have to live a perfect life, thereby, keeping the Law in every respect, but, as well, the terrible sin debt, which included every human being who had ever lived, had piled higher and higher through the centuries. This debt had to be addressed, had to be paid, and had to be paid in full. For that to happen, which would atone for all sin, Jesus had to go to the Cross. He had to give His Life because His Life was a Perfect Life, which He gave by the shedding of His Blood, which Peter referred to as *"Precious Blood"* (I Pet. 1:19).

God accepted the Sacrifice, meaning that Jesus had taken our place, and now sinful man could be justified.

HOW WAS MAN TO RECEIVE JUSTIFICATION?

Paul said, *"Therefore being justified by Faith, we have peace with God through our Lord Jesus Christ"* (Rom. 5:1).

So, what does it mean to be *"Justified by Faith"*?

In Chapters 4 and 5 of Romans, Paul goes to great length to portray to the human family that Justification is not at all obtained by works or merit but strictly by Faith.

He goes to this great length simply because there is something in man that seeks to earn his way with the Lord. It is a result of the Fall, but it is the biggest problem faced by the human family. We keep trying to do for ourselves what we cannot do; however, even if we could do it, that is, after a measure, God couldn't accept it because of our fallen condition. God can only accept what His Son and our Saviour, the Lord Jesus Christ, has done, and that alone!

WHAT DO WE MEAN *"BY FAITH"*?

It means that the believing sinner and the Christian, for that matter, must ever have Christ and the Cross as the Object of their Faith. Christ must not be separated from the Cross, and, of course, the Cross must not be separated from Christ. I'm sure the reader understands that we aren't speaking of the Cross as a wooden beam, but rather what Jesus there accomplished.

To evidence Faith in Christ and the Cross proclaims the fact that we firmly believe in what Christ did for us and accept it at face value (Jn. 3:16; Rom. 6:3-5; Eph. 2:13-18; Col. 2:10-15).

Incidentally, *"Faith"* is one ingredient, which can be utilized by anyone and everyone, irrespective of whom they might be or where they might be. It is the same for the young, the old, the rich, the poor, the sick, the well, etc. When we speak of Faith, always and without exception, it is Faith in Christ and what Christ did for us at the Cross.

Thank the Lord that Faith was chosen. If God had chosen something else, it would have left out certain segments of society, but Faith can be had by all!

So, when the believing sinner evidences Faith in Christ, believing what Jesus did for us at the Cross, at that moment, the Lord imputes to that individual a spotless Righteousness, which, in effect, means that one has been totally and completely justified.

As it concerns Justification by Faith, Paul said:

"For if by one man's offence *(Adam)* death reigned by one *(as a result of the Fall)*; much more they who receive **abundance of Grace and of the Gift of Righteousness** *(which we receive by accepting Christ and what He did for us at the Cross)* **shall reign** *(rule)* **in life by One,**

Jesus Christ.) *(Christ is the Source while the Cross is the Means)*" **(Rom. 5:17).**

CHRIST, THE CROSS, OUR FAITH, AND THE HOLY SPIRIT

Please note the following very carefully. Even though it is very much abbreviated, I think it explains the Great Plan of God, i.e., the New Covenant, which, in effect, is the Cross of Christ.

• Christ is the Source of all things we receive from God (Jn. 1:1, 14, 29; 3:16; 14:6; Col. 2:10-15).

• The Cross of Christ is the Means, and the only Means, by which these good things are given to us (I Cor. 1:17-18, 23; 2:2; Gal. 6:14).

• With the Cross of Christ being the Means by which these things are given to us, the Cross of Christ must ever be the Object of our Faith (Rom. 6:1-14; I Cor. 2:2; Col. 2:10-15).

• With our Faith properly placed in the Cross of Christ, and remaining in the Cross of Christ, the Holy Spirit, Who works exclusively within the parameters, so to speak, of the Finished Work of Christ, and Who will not work outside of those boundaries, will then work mightily on our behalf, making us what we ought to be, which He Alone can do (Rom. 8:1-11; Eph. 2:13-18).

Jesus Christ is the New Covenant, and the Cross of Christ is the Meaning of that Covenant.

So, David, the same as all, was justified solely on the basis of the Shed Blood of Christ, which cleanses from all sin (I Jn. 1:9).

DAVID'S PRAYER OF REPENTANCE

I think it would be good at this juncture to portray David's prayer of Repentance, which, as we shall see, was far more than just this one man. It did the following:

• It dealt with David and his sin.

• It portrays, in essence, the prayer that Israel will pray when she comes to Christ at the Second Coming.

• It also serves as the Intercessory Work of Christ all on our behalf.

"Have Mercy upon me, O God, according to Your Loving-kindness: according unto the multitude of Your Tender Mercies blot out my transgressions" (Ps. 51:1).

This is a Psalm of David, written when Nathan the Prophet came unto him after the sin with Bath-sheba and the murder of her husband Uriah (II Sam., Chpt. 12). This Psalm was given by the Holy Spirit to David when, his heart broken and contrite because of his sin against God, he pleaded for pardon through the atoning Blood of the Lamb of God, foreshadowed in Exodus, Chapter 12. Thus, he was not only fittingly provided with a vehicle of expression in Repentance and Faith, but he was also used as a channel of prophetic communication.

A FOREPICTURE OF ISRAEL

David, in his sin, Repentance, and Restoration, is a forepicture of Israel, for as he forsook the Law and was guilty of adultery and murder, so Israel despised the Covenant, turned aside to idolatry (spiritual adultery), and murdered the Messiah.

Thus, the scope and structure of this Psalm goes far beyond David. It predicts the future confession and forgiveness of Israel in the day of the Messiah's Second Coming, when looking upon Him Whom they pierced, they shall mourn and weep (Zech., Chpts. 12-13).

THE INTERCESSORY WORK OF CHRIST

As well, this is even more perfectly a vivid portrayal of the Intercessory Work of Christ on behalf of His People, which includes every Believer, both Jew and Gentile. Even though David prayed this prayer, the Son of David would make David's sin (as well as ours) His Own and pray through him that which must be said.

This means that this is the truest prayer of Repentance ever prayed because it symbolizes the Intercessory Work of the Son of David, all on our behalf.

WASH AND CLEANSE ME

"Wash me thoroughly from my iniquity, and cleanse me from my sin" (Ps. 51:2).

Man's problem is sin, and man must admit that. The only remedy for sin is *"Jesus Christ and Him Crucified,"* to which David, in essence, appealed (Heb. 10:12). The Blood of Jesus Christ alone cleanses from all sin (I Jn. 1:7).

THE ACKNOWLEDGMENT OF SIN

"For I acknowledge my transgressions: and my sin is ever before me" (Ps. 51:3).

The acknowledgement of Verses 3 through 4 is the condition of Divine forgiveness. All sin, in essence, is committed against God; therefore, God demands that the transgressions be acknowledged, placing the blame where it rightfully belongs—on the perpetrator. He cannot and, in fact, will not forgive sin that is not acknowledged and for which no responsibility is taken.

OUR SIN IS AGAINST GOD

"Against You, You only, have I sinned, and done this evil in Your Sight: that You might be justified when You speak, and be clear when You judge" (Ps. 51:4)

While David's sins were against Bath-sheba, her husband Uriah, and all of Israel, still, the ultimate direction of sin, perfected by Satan, is always against God.

All sin is a departure from God's Ways to man's ways.

David is saying that God is always *"justified"* in any action that He takes, and His *"Judgment"* is always Perfect.

ORIGINAL SIN

"Behold, I was shaped in iniquity; and in sin did my mother conceive me" (Ps. 51:5).

Unequivocally, this Verse proclaims the fact of original sin. This Passage states that all are born in sin as a result of Adam's fall in the Garden of Eden.

When Adam, as the federal head of the human race, failed, this means that all of humanity failed. It means that all who would be born would, in effect, be born lost.

As a result of this, the Second Man, the Last Adam, the Lord Jesus Christ, had to come into this world, in effect, God becoming Man, to undo what the original Adam did. He would have to keep the Law of God perfectly, which He did, all as our Substitute. He would then have to pay the penalty for the terrible sin debt owed by all of mankind, for all had broken the Law. He did this by giving Himself on the Cross of Calvary (Jn. 3:16).

To escape the Judgment of original sin, man must be *"Born-Again,"* which is carried out by the believing sinner expressing Faith in Christ and what Christ did at the Cross (Jn. 3:3; Eph. 2:8-9).

TRUTH IN THE INWARD PARTS

"Behold, You desire truth in the inward parts: and in the hidden part You shall make me to know wisdom" (Ps. 51:6).

Man can only deal with the externals, and even that, not very well. God Alone can deal with the *"inward parts"* of man, which is the source of sin, which speaks of the heart. In other words, the heart has to be changed, which the Lord Alone can do (Mat. 5:8).

WHITER THAN SNOW

"Purge me with hyssop, and I shall be clean: wash me, and I shall be whiter than snow" (Ps. 51:7).

The petition, *"Purge me with hyssop,"* expresses a figure of speech. *"Purge me with the blood, which on that night in Egypt was sprinkled on the doorposts with a bunch of hyssop"* (Ex. 12:13, 22), portrays David's dependence on *"the Blood of the Lamb."*

David had no recourse in the Law, even as no one has recourse in the Law. The Law can only condemn. All recourse is found exclusively in Christ and what He did for us at the Cross, of which the slain lamb and the blood on the doorposts in Egypt were symbols (Ex. 12:13).

HEALING

"Make me to hear joy and gladness; that the bones which You have broken may rejoice" (Ps. 51:8).

Forgiveness for the past never exhausts the fullness of pardon. There is provision for the future.

The expression, *"Bones which You have broken,"* presents a figure of speech meaning that one cannot proceed until things have been made right with God. It is as though a man's leg is broken, and he cannot walk. Unforgiven sin immobilizes the soul the same as a broken bone immobilizes the body.

BLOT OUT ALL MY INIQUITIES

"Hide Your Face from my sins, and blot out all my iniquities" (Ps. 51:9).

Unforgiven sin stares in the Face of God. This can only be stopped when the sins are put away, which can only be done by proper confession and Repentance, with the Blood of Jesus being applied by Faith. When this is done, the *"iniquities"* are *"blotted out"* as though they had never existed. This is *"Justification by Faith"* (Rom. 5:1).

A RIGHT SPIRIT

"Create in me a clean heart, O God; and renew a right spirit within me" (Ps. 51:10).

David's heart was unclean. Sin makes the heart unclean. The word *"create"* is interesting. It means the old heart is infected by sin, is diseased, and cannot be salvaged. God must, spiritually speaking, *"create a clean heart"* (Ezek. 18:31).

Also, it is impossible for any individual to have a *"right spirit"* if there is unconfessed sin.

TAKE NOT YOUR HOLY SPIRIT FROM ME

"Cast me not away from Your Presence; and take not Your Holy Spirit from me" (Ps. 51:11).

If sin is unconfessed and rebellion persists, God will ultimately *"cast away"* the individual *"from His Presence."* He will also *"take the Holy Spirit"* from the person. This refutes the doctrine of Unconditional Eternal Security.

RESTORATION

"Restore unto me the joy of Your Salvation; and uphold me with Your Free Spirit" (Ps. 51:12).

Part of the business of the Holy Spirit is *"Restoration,"* but only if the individual meets God's Conditions, as David did, and as we must do. With unconfessed sin, all *"joy"* is lost. With sin confessed, cleansed, and put away, the *"joy of Salvation"* returns. A clean heart, a willing spirit, and a steadfast will are then given by the Holy Spirit.

THE WAYS OF THE LORD

"Then will I teach transgressors Your Ways; and sinners shall be converted unto You" (Ps. 51:13).

Before Repentance, David was in no condition to proclaim God's Truth to *"transgressors,"* because he was a transgressor himself.

Upon true Repentance, David was now ready to teach and to preach, and the Holy Spirit attested to that.

BLOOD GUILTINESS

"Deliver me from blood guiltiness, O God, You God of my

Salvation: and my tongue shall sing aloud of Your Righteousness" (Ps. 51:14).

This refers to the terrible sin of having Uriah, the husband of Bath-sheba, killed (II Sam. 11:14-21).

Only the consciously pardoned sinner can *"sing aloud"* of God's Righteousness. Unpardoned men can speak of His Mercy, but their thoughts about it are unholy thoughts.

PRAISING THE LORD

"O LORD, open You my lips; and my mouth shall show forth Your Praise" (Ps. 51:15).

Proper praise to the Lord cannot go forth as long as there is unconfessed sin. This is the reason for such little praise in most churches, and far too often, the praise, which actually is offered, is hollow. True praise can only come from a true heart!

ONLY THE CROSS OF CHRIST

"For You desire not sacrifice; else would I give it: You delight not in Burnt Offering" (Ps. 51:16).

No penance, sacraments, or costly gifts of churches or men, regarding expiation of past sins, is desired or accepted by God. Only Faith and trust in Christ and what He has done for us at the Cross can be accepted by the Lord.

Unfortunately, the world tries to create a new god while the church tries to create another sacrifice. There is only one Sacrifice for sin (Heb. 10:12).

A BROKEN SPIRIT

"The sacrifices of God are a broken spirit: a broken and a contrite heart, O God, You will not despise" (Ps. 51:17).

True Repentance will always include a *"broken spirit"* and a *"broken and contrite heart."* Such alone will accept Christ and what Christ has done at the Cross. God will accept nothing less.

RESTORE ISRAEL

"Do good in Your Good Pleasure unto Zion: build You the walls of Jerusalem" (Ps. 51:18).

Verses 18 and 19 are not, as some think, a meaningless addition to the Psalm by some later writer. They both belong to the structure and prophetic scope of the Psalm.

David's sin, confession, and Restoration illustrate this future chapter in Israel's history. With their idolatry (spiritual adultery) and murder forgiven, they will go forth as Messengers of the Gospel to win other nations to wholehearted Faith and service in and for Christ.

Upon Israel's Repentance, the Lord will once again *"build You the walls of Jerusalem."*

THE ALTAR

"Then shall You be pleased with the sacrifices of Righteousness, with Burnt Offering and Whole Burnt Offering: then shall they offer bullocks upon Your Altar" (Ps. 51:19).

The sacrificial program under the old system was lawful because it pointed to the coming Redeemer. Since Christ and the Cross, they are no longer necessary, and for all the obvious reasons. Why the Symbol when the Substance is available?

During the Millennial Reign, the Sacrificial system will be restored, but only as a memorial of what Christ has done at the Cross (Ezek., Chpts. 40-48).

Now we will return to the Restoration of Israel, which will take place immediately after the Second Coming.

DAVID, THE KING FOREVER

"And they shall dwell in the land that I have given unto Jacob My Servant, wherein your fathers have dwelt; and they shall dwell therein, even they, and their children, and their children's children forever: and My Servant David shall be their

prince forever" (Ezek. 37:25).

This Passage goes back to the Messianic Promise of II Samuel 7:12-16. Some have concluded that the name *"David"* refers to the Messiah; however, the Holy Spirit uses the phrase, *"My Servant David,"* but never once is Christ called *"My Servant David."* So, it is obvious that king David is the one predicted here to be *"their prince forever."*

Actually, David will have a Glorified Body and will serve under Christ, with our Lord at that time, and we continue to speak of the Kingdom Age, actually serving as the President of the entire world, i.e., *"King of kings and Lord of lords."*

THE EVERLASTING COVENANT

"Moreover I will make a Covenant of Peace with them; it shall be an Everlasting Covenant with them: and I will place them, and multiply them, and will set My Sanctuary in the midst of them forevermore" (Ezek. 37:26).

The setting of the *"Divine Sanctuary"* in Jerusalem will cause the heathen to know that God has especially chosen Israel for His Peculiar Treasure. This Sanctuary is described in Chapters 40 through 48 of the Book of Ezekiel.

This *"Everlasting Covenant"* is all based on what Jesus did at the Cross, which, in effect, is the very meaning of the New Covenant, i.e., *"Everlasting Covenant."* This Covenant is based on better Promises than all the other Covenants (Heb. 8:6-13), and, in fact, is a perfect Covenant, which means it will never have to be amended.

THE TABERNACLE

"My Tabernacle also shall be with them: yes, I will be their God, and they shall be My People" (Ezek. 37:27).

This *"Tabernacle"* refers to an ozone type of covering, much greater than presently, which will be during the Millennium, when the light of the sun will be increased sevenfold and the light of the moon will be as the present light of the sun (Isa. 4:5).

WHEN THE LORD SANCTIFIES ISRAEL

"And the heathen shall know that I the LORD do sanctify Israel, when My Sanctuary shall be in the midst of them forevermore" (Ezek. 37:28).

God's Presence with Israel is the sign that He is with them and that the world must and, in fact, will recognize this approval.

Thus we see the outcome of the Battle of Armageddon. It will not turn out at all as the Antichrist and his unholy sponsor, Satan, had anticipated. It will conclude with Satan, plus all his fallen Angels and demon spirits, being thrown into the bottomless pit, where they will remain for a thousand years and then be transferred to the Lake of Fire (Rev. 20:1-3, 10). As well, the Beast (the Antichrist) and the False Prophet will be instantly thrown into Hell and then, ultimately, to the Lake of Fire where they *". . . shall be tormented day and night forever and ever"* (Rev. 20:10).

"Though the angry surges roll,
"On my tempest-driven soul,
"I am peaceful, for I know,
"Wildly though the winds may blow,
"I've an anchor safe and sure,
"That can evermore endure."

"Mighty tides about me sweep,
"Perils lurk within the deep,
"Angry clouds o'er-shade the sky,
"And the tempest rises high;
"Still I stand the tempest's shock,
"For my anchor grips the Rock."

"I can feel the anchor fast,
"As I meet each sudden blast,

"And the cable, though unseen,
"Bears the heavy strain between,
"Through the storm I safely ride,
"'Till the turning of the tide."

"Troubles almost overwhelm the soul;
"Griefs like billows o'er me roll;
"Tempters seek to lure astray;
"Storms obscure the light of day:
"But in Christ I can be bold,
"I've an anchor that shall hold."

Bibliography

CHAPTER 9
John Rosenstern, *The Land Is Mine: Part I & II; The Evangelist*, July & August Issues, 2011.

NOTES

NOTES

NOTES

NOTES

NOTES